*"Spirituality is a deeper involvement with life; so deep that the Creator reveals his own creation. A spiritual journey begins with aspiration and completes with realization.* During the course of this journey our *Inner dialogue reflects the fire of our soul with our intentions having infinite organizing power. As we let our soul take charge then enlightenment makes a secret handshake."*

- Vincent Keny, PhD

We have seen Vincent religiously working on this book over the last one year. - This book happens to be a spiritual tool kit, easy to understand and practice, leading towards personal transformation.

- Souls who know Vincent closely

# About The Author

Vincent Keny is an Indian people development professional, Master Trainer, Executive Coach, Keynote Speaker & Author. A committed Vedantic practioner, a firm believer in Universal Consciousness and apassionate follower of Swami Vivekananda, Vincent also has been initiated at Ramakrishna Mission Belur Math, Kolkata.

Vincent is awarded a place in the 100 Top Global Training Minds by World HRD Congress.

**Social Life:**

A personal transformation coach on body-mind-soul relationship. A voluntary speaker and mentor for Breast Cancer Awareness Interventions. A spiritual therapist with an aim to achieving a higher state of consciousness and teaching others how to achieve theirs.

**Academic & Professional credentials:**

Executive General Management Excellence Program (EGMEP) -

MIIT - Sloan School of Executive Education

Ph.D. Organisational Psychology, University of Oneida, New York, US

M.A. Cognitive Sciences, University of Allahabad

B.A. Hons Psychology, University of Delhi

Graduated St.Columbas School, New Delhi – '98 Batch

Certified Trainer of Emotional Intelligence, Talent Smart Inc, San Diego, US

Certified Trainer of LIFO Method Orientations, The Schutz Company, NY, US

Certified Trainer of Situational Leadership II (SLX Version), Ken Blanchard, US

Associated Certified Coach with International Coach Federation (ACC, ICF)

Certified NLP Practitioner (Dr. Richard Bandler's Society of NLP), US Certified Train The Trainer, XLRI, Jamshedpur, India

# The Fire of the Soul

Vincent Keny, PhD

ZORBA BOOKS

**ZORBA BOOKS**

Publishing Services in India by Zorba Books, 2019

Website: www.zorbabooks.com
Email: info@zorbabooks.com

Copyright © Vincent Keny, PhD

ISBN 978-93-88497-64-0
E-Book ISBN 978-93-88497-65-7

**Zorba Books Pvt. Ltd.(opc)**
Gurgaon, INDIA

Dedicated to my mother's soul.

Reverence to all souls who have contributed to this
book directly as well as indirectly.
To my children Sarah & Samar and my nieces Kirsa,
Kiana & Shanaya, with
blessings and good wishes for their spiritual
awakenings.

# Content

# Acknowledgement

My sincere thanks to space, time & events in my life that inspired me to write this book. It is the synchrodestiny that you as reader and this book came across each other.

# From the Author

My sincere thanks and gratitude to the reader for sharing my thoughts. I hope it will add value to some areas of your life. I have simply pened down my free-flowing spiritual experiences. I have just shared what I feel in every moment of my life. It is like a bird that just sings the song in the air and leaves its symphony for anyone to pick up or enjoy. The basic purpose of our lives is to discover who we are and the moment we understand who we are, the rest of the mystery of life unfolds itself and is revealed to us.

Everything in life is an expression of the miraculous unfolding of spirit. In every moment, the spirit just unfolds spontaneously, and the universe evolves into higher levels of creativity, awareness, and divinity.

True success is to witness the unfolding of the divinity within us. It is the perception of divinity wherever we go, in whatever we perceive – in the eyes of a child, in the beauty of a flower, in the flight of a bird. When we experience every moment of our lives as the miraculous expression of divinity, then we know the true meaning of success. We are travelers on a cosmic journey, and this moment is a little parenthesis in eternity. Life is eternal, but the expressions of life are momentary and transient. Buddha once said, "This existence of ours is as transient as autumn clouds. A lifetime is like a flash of lightning in the sky, rushing by like a torrent down a steep mountain."

We have stopped for a moment to encounter one another, to meet, to love, to share. If we share with caring, lightheartedness and love, we will create abundance and joy for one another. And then this moment will have been worthwhile.

The whole universe is played out inside us; we are not a drop in the ocean, we are the entire ocean itself carrying several drops. Every relationship that we hold in this world is the reflection of our oneness. We should be alert, awake to the coincidences and know that they are messages from cosmic intelligence and we must flow with the cosmic dance.

Let's be mindful about the the higher consciousness that we say is driving events, is consciousness and our consciousness is identified with and is encompassed by that same universal consciousness. When we know our individual will to be unified with the cosmic will, then events are no longer happening to us, we are participating in the co-creation of these events.

Being a dedicated Vedic follower and a secure believer in Universal Consciousness as well as Yogic practices; I have made an honest attempt to share my experiential *way of being* that I experience as a silent witness to my Self. Know one thing by which everything else is known, that is Consciousness

A sincere dedication, with reverence, to all the souls who have contributed to this book directly as well as indirectly.

Once again, I appreciate your kindness for the courtesy extended to read this book.

Stay Blessed.

Vincent Vinayak Keny, PhD

# Power of Silent Witness

There is no reason why understanding how to awaken your soul should be difficult or painful. Nature is always orchestrating situations around us to bring about self-realization. When we attune ourselves to these whispers and the synchronicity of the universe around us, the process becomes fun and smooth. If we do not notice or listen, nature is compelled to raise the volume to try to get through to us. This presents itself as more dramatic, extreme and sometimes painful experiences. During our spiritual journey, it is important that we do not try to impose an ideal behavior or attitude over our present experience. The emotional and mental strain only adds to our pain and discomfort. If we are in deep emotional pain or grief, the way forward to self-awareness is to be with the pain, not to pretend it isn't there or it isn't real. We need to concentrate our attention on the experience in its raw form, without allowing the mind's story of how it happened, who's at fault, whether it's unfair or unkind and what it will take to stop it, to interrupt the experience. We need to be with the experience without judgment, neither agreeing nor disagreeing with it.

Often, the best way to do this is to observe the physical sensation associated with the emotional experience and then let your attention remain with that sensation. You can connect your breath with the sensation if you like in order to help your mind stay in the present experience and prevent it from wandering or returning to old stories and judgments. In a little while, the sensation will diminish and fade away and you will feel the emotional pain getting lighter or dissipating entirely. Now, you are back in a state of balance where you can more effectively use other spiritual powers. Your thoughts are in you, you are not in your thoughts. You are not the experience, but you are the experiencer. You are not the knowledge, but you are the knower.

The Self is the prime core of your being from where everything originates for conception. The Self is nothing but the soul consciousness that is an extension of the universal consciousness. The Self transcends space, time, event or causality. The self is neither born, nor will it die, being eternal it will only transform. A change takes place in daily actions/behavior when you live from the soul instead of taking the conditioned ego mind as a reference point. It actually turns into non-doing, which is the same as consenting. You step aside and let your soul act through you, without any struggle, worry, resistance or anticipation. Non-doing is not the same as doing nothing. Rather, it is the most powerful way to live life because your soul wants to bring about the best possible outcome for you. Your role is to tune in and witness how perfectly life can organize itself when the soul is in charge. Here, we become light-minded, willingly open to forgiving and seeking forgiveness, compassionate, joyful, and blissful. Equanimity becomes your everyday conduct. Hence, we experience all the support from the universe. The soul is a cosmic connector between local and non-local self. Once there is an absolute surrender to universal consciousness, wherein soul becomes the prime driver, the "state of grace" begins. Soul is the core Self, the source of everything – including our thoughts and the most basic thinking (Meta-cognition), imagination, intentions and desires. When our intentions and desires become the intents/desires of the entire universe, it orchestrates and manifests them through the cosmic plan with more ease and grace.

If anger arises and you try to manage it, this implies that a part of you is attempting to improve another part. However, there is only one self so this division is very problematic. If you are trying to improve your self-esteem, why would you call upon yourself to achieve this goal unless a part of you already has better self-esteem?

These aren't simple questions. Living with a divided self has been a situation addressed in psychiatry, religion, and social relations in general. Humans are conflicted inside, which leads to conflicts outside. So, the deeper aim of relating to oneself is to heal self-division and achieve wholeness.

You have to undo the build-up of these negative states, which typically develop over many years beginning in childhood. If you build an unstable house, you can go back and fix it. But an unsteady sense of self feels like who you are. Unfortunate traits have become embedded in your sense of self. Once you see this, it becomes complicated to undo the things about yourself that you don't like.

It's not clear whether the divided self is capable of healing itself. People who seriously give it a try through psychotherapy or self-help discover very quickly that you cannot pull one thread from a ball of story. In order to solve this dilemma, I think meditation and mindfulness are a good start. Going beneath the restless surface activity of the mind is the initial point of meditation. Watching yourself as you act in the world is the point of mindfulness. These are both good things.

But techniques alone won't solve inner conflict, confusion, and division. There has to be a committed intention to move beyond the divided self. Once you realize that you can't pull one thread out, you also come to the realization that you have to do something about the whole ball of story. This goes beyond relying upon an age-old belief that there is such a thing as waking up. In other words, you can go beyond the divided self and all its problems to arrive at a higher state of awareness, whether you call it enlightenment, non-dualism, or the state of oneness. Regardless of name, the project of waking up involves exploring your own consciousness. Once this begins to interest you, the journey away from the divided self has begun. "If you don't know what to fix up, what will you fix up?"

Yes, it is the silent awareness that shifts its attention inward on itself instead of outward through the senses and objects of perception. It is the one inside you that is listening and observing all that you think, feel and do. The inner witness can be self-referral and therefore conscious of itself. That is why the presence of the self is called consciousness – it knows itself through itself and by itself. In this way, it becomes awakened to its full potentiality.

The silent witness is your essential nature. As your consciousness awakens, and you experience greater clarity, you begin to become aware of who you are— that is the "ME" in that state of consciousness. When awareness is not aware of its real nature, then your sense of identity is attached to the memories, conditioning, perceptions and feelings of the ego mind. In that state of consciousness, the ego-mind is the "ME". So, your sense of self or identity is not so much a matter of choice as it is an automatic reflection of your state of consciousness.

As your consciousness becomes clearer, more awake to itself, it comes to the knowledge of its true nature."

The spiritual value that can come out of this process is for you to learn to shift your perspective from the ego personality to the universal silent witness awareness. That is the real experience of detachment. Some believe that manifestation is merely a matter of understanding the power of attraction and applying the mechanics of visualization and affirmation so that the universe delivers what your ego wants, when it wants it. But in my experience, the deeper secret of creativity is to cultivate the awakening of consciousness to its true status as abundance, joy, and all possibilities, so that the ego expands to become the universe and then every desire becomes the desire of the universe. This has the benefit of the entire cosmos working for you, and additionally, you remain fulfilled and complete at every step of the process.

For those who might be unfamiliar with these ideas, the basic idea behind the power of attraction is that thoughts have a power or energy that can attract similar energy. If you know what you want, ask for it, are receptive to it and behave as if it's coming, then it will come. The Sanskrit word *karma* literally means action--all kinds of action, intended and unintended action on mental, physical, emotional and spiritual levels. The power of karma tells us that those actions have commensurate consequences in time, both in the short term and the long term.

The power of karma is based on the principles of attraction. It is suggested that intention creates effect—your intended outcome. Attention energizes and intention transforms. However, the power of attraction doesn't factor in the preexisting effects of your past thoughts and behavior on your present desires.

We don't enter this life as a blank slate. We come in with our own particular history and past tendencies, which circumscribe what we are likely to manifest, regardless of how fervently we practice the powers of attraction. For instance, if you do not have the required educational background in the field of Medicine, and at age 40 you suddenly desire to become a surgeon in a hospital, it's not going to happen no matter how positive your thoughts are. The present karma in place that is playing out makes this possibility an impractical use of your attention. The power of attraction works as an effective tool of manifestation when one has determined that the other karmic factors are already favorable and if they are not, they are minor enough that they can be overcome with some diligence and discipline.

Subtle Intentions are the most powerful intentions, they are the innermost faint voice which is deep, delicate, intuitive. They create a ripple effect since they arise out of contentment rather than need/want when the mind is in a clam state.

Inherent in every intention and desire is the mechanics for its fulfillment; intention and desire in the field of pure potentiality have infinite organizing power. And when we introduce an intention in the fertile ground of pure potentiality, we put this infinite organizing power to work for us. We need to trust the cosmic plan and let cosmic intelligence work on the details. Henceforth, it will lead to its orchestration, manifestation and fulfilment at the appropriate time. Expectancy determines the outcome till the time we are detached from the outcome. The outcome is guaranteed. Enjoy the journey blissfully and the rest will be like the pieces of a puzzle fitting together. Of course, needless to mention the intent and desire should be to the benefit of humanity and mankind. In case you are in a state of confusion, the only source of internal referral should be your "SOUL" and not your "conditioned mind". It should not be your created social self-image that we know by the name of "EGO". You need to follow the inner voice that comes from your heart, as it is your cosmic computer. It will surely guide you if you connect to it with the matching frequency. Each and every cell in the body taps the inner voice.

I understand the point that the way we structure our intentions influences the way our goals are manifested. If we are coming from a place of lack based on lack of self-awareness, then we will not find satisfaction through our wants and desires. I feel strongly that we need to become the change that we want to achieve. Therefore, we create peace around us by being a lighthouse of peace in our own lives. It is this simple version of wanting peace that I am talking about. Because the expansion of peace is coming from the fullness of inner peace, there is no lack anywhere.

# Power of Desire

Desires comes spontaneously from the unknown. When we effortlessly put our attention on them, settle into being, and leave the results to the unknown, they mysteriously get fulfilled. Everything is caused by numerable factors of which our personal effort is only one. We are just one link in the chain of causation. This is the magic of the human mind when we desire and let go. Step into the unknown in every moment in your life and you will be free. When we speak of dreams coming true, we are talking about some form of desire. Beyond the basic necessities for food, water, and shelter, which are enough to satisfy the need to survive, human beings invent countless other desires. We all experience some of our desires becoming fulfilled, while others don't. That seems clear enough. However, people approach this simple fact from very different angles. If asked, "How do you get what you want?" or, "How do you make a dream come true?" people will offer answers that aren't at all compatible. Think of the mixed messages we've been getting all our lives:

- *Desires are fulfilled, and dreams become reality if you work hard enough and never stop fighting for what you want.*

- *Dreams get fulfilled only if they are meant to. It hardly matters what you do; destiny or karma plays the major role.*

- *It's pure luck which desires get fulfilled and which don't.*

- *Making your dreams become reality is a spiritual journey. Prayer, meditation, and good karma are critical.*

- *Dreams get fulfilled by the grace of God. To make your dream become reality, you must surrender to divine will.*

- *Desire is self-fulfilling. Every intention includes a path to fulfillment within its structure, however remote fulfillment might seem to be.*

- *Getting what you want is inevitable, but you have to look deep enough. Fulfillment can occur on the level of fantasy, dream, or imagination. It doesn't have to be physical.*

Our tendency is to pick and choose from these explanations, and as a result, the picture of desire gets more confused than ever. Fulfilling a desire could require hard work or the opposite, total surrender. If something wonderful falls into your lap, does it matter if God or random chance caused it? These appear to be exact opposites. Yet, one of the traditional sources of wisdom in India, the Bhagavad-Gita, fuses opposites when Lord Krishna says, "Perform action without attachment to the fruits of action." In other words, use focus, determination, and hard work all you want, but stay detached about the outcome. In that dictum, a commitment to action and surrender to the outcome are fused.

Why is this a wise strategy? In our daily life, we're all attached to the outcome of desire. We want the paycheck, the girl/boy, the raise, the nice house. Focusing on those desires without caring about the outcome doesn't seem like wisdom. It seems self-defeating. We need to go back to the common experience of having a desire. Let's say three people want a piece of chocolate cake. Person A goes to work and earns enough money to buy a chocolate cake. Person B comes home to discover that coincidentally, his wife has baked a chocolate cake for him. Person C orders chocolate cake at a restaurant only to be told that the last piece was already sold!

The unlikely truth is that all three desires operated by the same mechanism in consciousness. This mechanism is intention working towards a conclusion. Despite the fact that an actual piece of cake appears—or doesn't—the entire mechanics of desire takes place in the consciousness. Why don't people see this automatically and accept it as a fact? Why don't we expect our desires to become reality without hindrance or struggle, letting fulfillment unfold through consciousness alone? The inner track of desire is masked because a person's consciousness varies enormously according to many factors: To be effortlessly fulfilled, an intention must be clear. Mixed messages bring mixed results. We send out mixed messages because of hidden beliefs and self-assumptions that muddy the waters (such as, "I don't deserve to get what I want" or "It's sinful to want too much" or "God wants me to be pure and without desire".)

Some intentions come from a shallow level that has no way to fulfillment. The deeper the desire, the stronger the intention. Intentions can take a direct path but also many indirect ones. Intention will reach a conclusion unless blocked or thwarted, but we can't control the conclusion or predict what path it will take — this is why detachment is necessary ultimately. There are so many variables in even the simplest desire, the mind is simply unable to calculate them all. All three people, persons A, B, and C, in the example wanted a piece of chocolate cake. They followed the same mechanics of desire but got three different results, and now we see why. Their intention was the same, but their inner world wasn't. Your awareness is like a filter through which a desire must pass, or better said, awareness is a maze of twisted turns that intentions must negotiate. Therefore, the Gita's advice to remain detached isn't just a snippet of ancient wisdom. It's practical advice, which can be literally stated as "Let the mechanics of desire bring your fulfillment without interference. The more you interfere, the less likely you will get what you want."

Follow your dream but remember this: desire is the universe's evolutionary tool. This is a clear-eyed statement, reflecting what we all experience. The self discloses itself over a lifespan through growing desires, moving from infancy to adulthood. Detachment occurs naturally as childish things no longer possess any charm and the desires of childhood, adolescence, and adulthood make new claims. Finally, one arrives at the mature adult who can formulate a vision of life and aspire to spiritual understanding. Then the track of desire and the track of consciousness both come to fruition.

Our essential nature which is in perfect attunement with the universe, knows exactly what we need at exactly the right time. The important factor in asking the universe to get what we need is not in the specificity of the desire, but letting go of the desire and returning to our unbounded awareness which is the place where the universe responds from.

# Power of Letting Go – Surrendering to a higher being

Every time you are tempted to react in the same old way, ask yourself if you want to be a prisoner of the past or a pioneer of the future. The past is closed and limited, the future is open and free. In practical terms, surrendering means letting go. Although you don't realize it, reality isn't a given. Each of us inhabits a separate reality. Your mind maintains your personal version of reality by buttressing it with beliefs, expectations, and interpretations. Your mind blocks the free flow of the life force by saying, "This is how things must and should be." Letting go releases you from the insistent grip, and when you let go, new forms of reality can enter.

You only have to take a ride on a roller coaster to see who gets more enjoyment out of the experience, those who clutch tight with white knuckles and clenched jaws or those who let go and allow themselves to be carried up and down without resistance.

Letting go is a process. You have to know when to apply it, what to let go of, and how to let go. Your mind is not going to show you any of these things. In fact, your ego will try to prevent you from making progress since it believes that you have to hold on in order to survive. Your only ally in letting go is spirit, which sees reality as a whole and therefore, has no need to create partial realities based on limitation.

The whole path to love could be described as learning to let go but letting go all at once isn't possible. This is a process that has many small steps. At any given moment, the steps are basically the same: awareness begins to substitute for reactions. A reaction is automatic. It draws upon fixed beliefs and expectations, images of past pain and pleasure residing in memory, waiting to guide you in future situations.

Overcoming any reaction requires an act of awareness. Awareness doesn't resist the imprint of memory. It sifts through your memories and questions whether you need older imprints/patterns for the current situation. For instance, if you are faced with a big dog, awareness tells you that you aren't a small child anymore and that not all big dogs bite. Being aware of this you can ask if you need to hold on to fear. Whether you wind up petting the dog, ignoring it, or withdrawing is now a matter of choice. Reactions result in a closed set of options, awareness results in an open set of options.

# When to let go

The critical times to let go are when you feel the strongest urge not to. We all hold on tightest when fear, anger, pride, and distrust take over. Yet, these forces have no spiritual validity. At those moments when you are afraid, angry, stubborn, or mistrustful, you are in the grip of unreality. Your ego is forcing you to react from the past, blinding you to new possibilities in the here and now.

Spirit has a good outcome for any situation, if you can open yourself to it.

# What to let go of

If the right time to let go is when you don't want to, the thing to let go of is the thing you feel you must hold on to. Fear, anger, stubbornness, and distrust portray themselves as your rescuers. Actually, these energies only make you more closed off. For example, panicky people tend to act that way because it is familiar. The same is true for angry and stubborn people. It is helpful to challenge familiar reactions by stating that you no longer believe in them. Here are a few examples:

Instead of saying "I have to have my way", say to yourself, "I don't know everything. I can accept an outcome I can't see right now". Instead of saying "I'm incredibly afraid", say to yourself "Fear isn't me". Being more afraid doesn't make it any more real. (This technique is also applicable to feelings of overwhelming anger, distrust, rejection, anxiety, and so forth).

## How to let go

Since letting go is a deeply personal choice you are going to have to be your own teacher. The process takes place on every level—physical, mental, emotional— where energy can be stuck or held and no two people have exactly the same issues. You might feel a lot more comfortable with physical release than someone else. I might feel a lot more comfortable with emotional release than you do. It is important to find the balance between physical, mental, and emotional release that works for you.

I also suggest that you embrace the following ideas as appropriate:

- This is just an experience. I'm here on earth to have experiences. Nothing is wrong.

- My higher Self knows what is going on. This situation is for my benefit, even if I can't see that now.

- My fears might come true, but the outcome will not destroy me. It may even be good. I'll wait and see.

- I'm having a strong reaction now, but it isn't the real me. It will pass.

- Whatever I am afraid of losing is meant to go. I will be better off when new energies come in. Whatever fear says, nothing can destroy me.

- When people fall they don't break, they bounce.

- Change is inevitable. Resisting change doesn't work.

- There is something here for me, if I have the awareness to find it.

- The things I fear the most have already happened. I don't want to hold on anymore. My purpose is to let go and welcome what is to come.

- Life is on my side.

- I am loved; therefore, I am safe.

**Learning to let go is like breathing.** With each breath, you inhale and exhale. You can't hold on to breath and if you do you will suffocate. Hence, the same thing will happen if you hold on to a thought, experience or emotion; just experience and let it go. Breath is a movement and not a thing. It just comes and goes as an experience. You are just the observer of the experience but not the experience itself. Breath is not a thing but movement being experienced in space and time but you, the observer, are beyond space, time and causation. There is little space/gap between the inflow and outflow of breath and this space or the gap is consciousness or pure potentiality.

I encourage you to embrace the coming season with a sense of openness, vitality, and a renewed sense of pure potentiality.

The power of pure potentiality is pure consciousness. It is the field of all possibilities and infinite creativity. Our physical body, the physical universe – everything in the material world – comes from the same place: a field of silent, unmoving, awareness from which anything is possible. There is no separation between this field of energy and our spiritual essence, our self. This field is our own self. And when we know that our essential nature is one of pure potentiality, we align with the power that manifests everything in the universe.

Knowing who we really are gives us the ability to fulfill any dream we have, because the same field that nature uses to create a forest, galaxy, or human body can also bring about the fulfillment of our desires. Anything is possible in the field of pure potentiality because this field is the source of all power, intelligence, and infinite organizing ability.

Therefore, success in life depends on knowing who we really are. When our internal reference point is our spirit, our true self, we experience all the power of our spirit. When our internal reference point is the ego or self-image, we feel cut off from our source, and the uncertainty of events create fear and doubt. The ego is influenced by objects outside the self—circumstances, people and things. It thrives on the approval of others. It wants to control, because it lives in fear. But the ego is not who we really are. The ego is our social mask. It is the role we are playing.

The need for approval, the need to control things, and the need for external power are fear based. This kind of power is not the power of pure potentiality, the power of the self or true power. Self- power is true power because it is based on the powers of nature and comes from the knowledge of the self. Self-power draws things that we want to us, it magnetizes people, situation and things to support our desires. This support from the powers of nature is the state of grace. When we are in harmony with nature, we create a bond between our own desires and the power to make these desires materialize.

How can you experience the power of pure potentiality? One way is through the practice of silence and meditation. This means tuning out the world and taking time to simply be. The following line appears in the book of Psalms, "Be still and know that I am God". Stillness is the first requirement for manifesting your desires, because you can connect with the field of pure awareness and infinite organizing power through stillness.

Imagine throwing a little stone into a still pond and watching the ripples that appear on the surface of the water. That's what you do when you enter silence and introduce your intention. Even the faintest intention ripples across the field of universal consciousness that connects your desires with everything else. This field can orchestrate an infinity of details for you. But if your mind is like a turbulent ocean, you could throw the empire state building into it and you wouldn't notice a thing.

Practicing non-judgement is another way to practice the power of pure potentiality. When you constantly judge things as right or wrong, good or bad, you create a lot of turbulence in your internal dialogue. This turbulence constricts the flow of energy between you and the field of pure potentiality. In the silent space between your thoughts is a state of pure awareness, an inner stillness that connects you to true power. Through the practice of non-judgement, you can silence your mind and access your inner stillness.

Another way to experience the power of pure potentiality is to spend time in nature. By observing nature, you begin to sense the harmonious interaction of all the elements and forces of life. The lavish display of abundance in the universe is an expression of the creative mind of nature. Just by tuning into nature, you will access the field of pure potentiality and infinite creativity, and spontaneously receive creative thoughts.

Whether it be a stream, a forest, a mountain or the sea, connecting with nature's intelligence will give you a sense of unity with all of life and help you to get in touch with the innermost essence of your being. This essence is full of magic and mystery. It is fearless, it is free. When you are grounded in the knowledge of your true self, you never feel fearful or insecure about money or fulfilling your desires. You never feel guilty about wanting many things or having an abundance of anything, because you realize that the essence of all material wealth is life energy. You know that your desires are inseparably connected with everything else. Your every desire is not your own. It's an evolutionary impulse coming through you, so why would you doubt it? That impulse is part of greater pattern, which will grow and evolve into greater abundance and creativity.

The pure potentiality says that you are consciousness itself, both as it manifests in the material world, and as it lies un-manifest in your being. With the knowledge and practice of this power, you can harmonize with nature and create with carefreeness, joy and love. Wherever you go in the midst of activity, carry your stillness within you. Then, the chaos around you will never overshadow your access to the field of pure potentiality.

Here are some suggestions to inculcate stillness within you:

- Take time each day to be silent, to connect with your spirit, to just be.

- Practice nonjudgement. Begin each day with the statement "Today I shall judge nothing that occurs" and throughout the day remind yourself of that statement each time you catch yourself judging something or someone.

- Commune with nature. Silently observe the intelligence within everything. Watch a sunset, listen to the sound of the ocean, or simply smell the scent of a flower.

# Power of Exchange Supremacy

Giving and receiving is based on the fact that everything in the universe operates through dynamic exchange. Every relationship is one of give and take because giving and receiving are different aspects of the flow of energy in the universe. If we stop the flow of energy, we interfere with nature's intelligence. We must give and receive in order to keep money, or anything we want, circulating in our lives.

Currency, our word for money, derives from a Latin word meaning "to run or flow". Money is a symbol of the life energy we give and receive as a result of the service we provide to others. Like a river, money must keep flowing, otherwise it begins to clog and stagnate. Circulation keeps it alive and vital. If we stop the circulation of life energy, if our intention is to hold on to our money and hoard it, we stop its circulation back into our lives.

The intention behind our giving and receiving is the most important thing. When the act of giving is joyful, when it is unconditional and from the heart, then the energy behind the giving increases many times over. But if we give grudgingly, there is no energy behind that giving. If we feel we have lost something through the act of giving, then the gift is not truly given and will not result in an increase.

The power of giving and receiving is simple: if you want love, learn to give love. If you want attention and appreciation, learn to give attention and appreciation. If you want material affluence, help others to become materially affluent. If you want to be blessed with all the good things in life, learn to silently bless everyone with all the good things in life. The more you give, the more you will receive. In your willingness to give that which you seek, you will keep the abundance of the universe circulating in your life.

Abundance has material expression, but what is really circulating is consciousness. Even the thought of giving, the thought of blessing or a simple prayer has the power to affect others. We are bundles of thought in a thinking universe and thought has the power to transform.

The best way to experience the power of giving and receiving is to give a gift to everyone you come into contact with. This doesn't have to be in the form of materials things. The gift of caring, affection, appreciation and love are some of the most precious gifts you can give and they don't cost you anything. One of the things I was taught as a child was never to go to anyone's house without taking a gift. You may say "How can I give to others when I don't have enough myself?" You can bring a note that says something about your feelings for the person you are visiting. You can bring a flower, a compliment or a prayer. Whenever you meet someone, silently send that person a blessing. This kind of silent giving is very powerful. Give wherever you go, and as you give, you will receive. As you receive, the more your ability to give will increase, and the more you'll gain confidence in the miraculous effects of this power.

There is nothing you lack because your essential nature is one of pure potentiality and infinite possibilities. You are inherently affluent no matter how much or how little money you have because the source of all wealth is the field of pure potentiality that knows how to fill every need.

Giving and receiving are nothing other than the flow of life—the harmonious interaction of all the elements and forces that structure the field of existence. The exchange of energy is a process that has its own timing, organization, and beauty. Your life unfolds in the same way. Everything that comes to you isn't something you earn, but a gift freely given by the universe, which means it comes from a deep awareness of what you need. Think of all the things that have been freely given to you without your having to ask for them. Just experiencing gratitude allows you to participate in the power of giving and receiving. Nature supports your every need and desire, including your need for joy, love, laughter, harmony and knowledge. Seek these things first—not only for yourself but for others—and all else will spontaneously come to you.

- Give a gift to everyone you encounter, be it a compliment, a flower, or a prayer. This will begin the process of circulating joy and affluence in your life and in the lives of others.

- Gratefully receive every gift that life offers you. Be open to receiving, whether it be a material gift from others, a compliment or a prayer.

- Silently wish everyone you encounter happiness, joy and laughter. By giving and receiving the gifts of caring and affection, appreciation and love, you will keep wealth circulating in your life.

# Power of Karmic Equilibrium

Karma is both action and the consequence of that action. Everyone has heard the expression "What you sow is what you reap". If we want to create happiness in our lives, we must learn to sow the seeds of happiness. Therefore, the power of karma implies the action of conscious choice making. When we choose actions that bring happiness and success to others, the fruit of our karma is happiness and success.

In every moment, we have access to an infinity of choices. Some choices are made consciously, while other are made unconsciously. Unfortunately, a lot of our choices are made unconsciously, and therefore we don't think they are choices – and yet they are. As a result of conditioning, our choices are often triggered by people and circumstances into predictable outcomes.

If I were to insult you, you would most likely make the choice of being offended. If I were to pay you a compliment, you would most likely make the choice of being flattered. But think about it: you could make the choice of not letting a compliment flatter you either.

The best way to use karmic power is to step back and witness the choices you are making in every moment. When you make any choice, ask yourself two things: "What are the consequences of this choice?" and "Will the choice I am making bring happiness to me and those around me?" There is always one choice that will create maximum happiness both for you and for those around you. This choice is spontaneous right action because it's the action that nourishes you and everyone else who is influenced by that action.

How do you make spontaneous right choices? By paying attention to sensations of comfort or discomfort in your body. At the moment you make a choice, ask your body, what are the consequences of this choice? If your body sends a message of comfort, that's the right choice. If you feel uneasiness in your body even as you ask the question, then it's not the appropriate choice.

For some people, the message of comfort or discomfort is in the area of the solar plexus, but for most people, it's the area of the heart. Concentrate on your heart and ask your heart what to do. Then, pay attention to how you feel. The response might be the faint, but it's there. You will know the answer is right because it will feel right, without any lingering doubts. The heart knows the correct answer because it taps into the field of pure potentiality and infinite organizing power and takes everything into account. The heart is intuitive and holistic. It has a win-win orientation. And though the answer may not seem rational, the heart is far more accurate than anything within the realm of rational thought.

You can use the power of karma to create money and the flow of all good things to you. But first, become aware of the choices that you are making in every moment. The more you become aware of choices, the more you will make choices that are spontaneously correct – both for you and for those around you.

How can you apply the power of karma to the choices you have already made? Most people pay their karmic debts – unconsciously, of course. Sometimes, there's a lot of suffering involved, but the power of karma says no debt in the universe ever goes unpaid.

If you want to transform your karma to a more desirable experience, look for the seed of opportunity within every adversity, and tie that seed of opportunity to your dharma or purpose in life. This will enable you to convert the adversity into benefit, and transform the karma into new expression.

Begin by asking yourself, "What message is the universe giving me? What can I learn from this experience and how can I make it useful to my fellow human beings?" For example, if you break your leg while playing sports, perhaps the message is that you need to slow down and be more attentive to your body. And if the purpose of your life is to teach others, ask, "What can I learn from this experience, and how can I make it useful to my fellow human beings?" You may decide to share what you have learnt by writing a book about playing sports safely. This transforms your karma into a positive experience.

You can also transcend the seeds of your karma by becoming independent of it. The way to do this is to keep experiencing the self, your spirit, by doing silent meditation. You will emerge anew. This is like washing a dirty piece of cloth in a stream of water. Each time you wash it, you take away a few stains and it gets a little cleaner.

Every action becomes a karmic episode because action generates memory, memory generates desire and desire generates action again. As you become conscious of these seeds of manifestation, you become a conscious choice maker, and the actions you generate will be evolutionary – both for you and for those around you – then the fruit of karma will be happiness and success.

- Witness the choices you make in every moment. The best way to prepare for any moment in the future is to be fully conscious in the present.

- Whenever you make a choice, ask yourself two questions: "What are the consequences of this choice?" and "Will this choice bring happiness to me and to those who are affected by this choice?"

- Ask your heart for guidance and be guided by its message of comfort and discomfort. If the choice feels comfortable, go ahead with that choice. If the choice feels uncomfortable, then don't make that choice.

# Power of Infinite Organizing Supremacy

Nature's intelligence functions with effortless ease, with carefreeness, harmony, and love. This is the principal of "do less and accomplish more". When we learn this lesson from nature, we easily fulfill our desires.

If we observe nature at work, we see that the least effort is expended. Grass doesn't try to grow; it just grows. Fish don't try to swim; they just swim. This is their intrinsic nature. It is the nature of the sun to shine. And it is human nature to make our dreams manifest into physical form – easily and effortlessly. What is commonly called ''miracle'' is actually an expression of the least effort.

Least effort is expended when our actions are motivated by love, because nature is held together by the energy of love. When we seek power and control over other people, we spend energy in a wasteful way. When we seek money for personal gain only, we cut off the flow of energy to ourselves, and interfere with the expression of nature's intelligence.

We waste our energy chasing the illusion of happiness instead of enjoying happiness in the moment. Attention to the whims of the ego consumes the greatest amount of energy. But when our internal reference point is our spirit, our actions are motivated by love, and there is no waste of energy. Our energy multiplies, and the surplus energy we gather can be channeled to create anything we want, including unlimited wealth. When we harness the power of harmony and love, we use our energy creatively for the experience of affluence and evolution.

How can you put the least effort into action? There are three things you can do. The first thing is to accept people, situations and events as they are, not as you wish them to be, in the moment. Any moment is as it should be because it took the entire universe to make the moment. When you struggle against the moment, you struggle against the entire universe. You can intend for things to be different in the future, but in the moment, accept things as they are.

The second thing is to take responsibility for your situation and for all the events you see as problems. This means not blaming anyone or anything for your situation, including yourself. Responsibility means the ability to have a creative response to any situation. All problems contain the seeds of opportunity and this awareness allows you to take the moment and transform it into a better situation.

If you do this, every upsetting situation becomes an opportunity for the creation of something new and beautiful, every tormentor or tyrant becomes your teacher. The relationships you have attracted in your life are precisely the ones you need at that moment. There is a hidden meaning behind all events that is contributing to your own evolution. And if you choose to interpret reality in this way, then you will have many teachers and many opportunities to evolve.

A third way to put the power of least effort into action is to practice defenselessness. This means relinquishing the need to convince others of your point of view. By doing this, you gain access to enormous amounts of energy that have previously been wasted.

When you have no point to defend, you stop fighting and resisting, and you can fully experience the present, which is a gift. When you embrace the present, you begin to experience the spirit within everything that is alive, and joy is born within you. As you drop the burden of defensiveness and resentment, you become lighthearted, joyous and free. In this joyful, simple freedom, you will know that what you want is available to you whenever you want it. This is because your want is coming from a state of happiness, not from a state of anxiety and fear.

The power of least effort assures us that there is always a simple, natural path to fulfilment. Nature's intelligence unfolds spontaneously through the path of least effort and no resistance. This is the way that you can live, too. When you combine acceptance, responsibility and defenselessness, your life flows with effortless ease. Your dreams and desires flow with nature's desires. Then you can release your intentions without attachment, and when the season is right, your desires will blossom into reality.

- Accept people, circumstances and events as they are in the moment. When confronted with any challenge, remind yourself, "This moment is as it should be", because the entire universe is at it should be.

- Take responsibility for your situation without blaming anything or anyone including yourself. Every problem is an opportunity to take the moment and transform it into greater benefit.

- Relinquish the need to defend your point of view. In defenselessness, you remain open to all points of view, not rigidly attached to one of them.

# Power of Intention

When released in the field of pure potentiality, intentions have infinite organizing power. Just by introducing an intention in the fertile ground of pure potentiality, we activate this field, and put its infinite organizing power to work for us. This isn't a mystical notion. Every time we have a desire to walk or lift our arms, our intention incites millions of chemical reactions and electrical impulses that obey fixed powers of nature. The fifth spiritual power says that inherent in every desire are the mechanics for its fulfilment, and these mechanics apply to desires reaching far beyond the physical body.

Energy and information exist everywhere in nature. At the level of pure consciousness, there is nothing other than energy and information. This means there are no well-defined edges between our physical body and our extended body – the universe. We can consciously change the energy and information of our own body, and influence the energy and information of our extended body – our environment – and cause things to manifest in it.

This change is bought about by two qualities inherent in consciousness: attention and intention. Attention energizes and intension transforms. Whatever we put our attention on grows stronger in our life; whatever we take our attention away from withers and disappears. Intention triggers the transformation of energy and information and organizes its own fulfilment. The quality of intention on the object of attention orchestrates an infinity of details to bring about the intended outcome.

We see the expression of this organizing power in every blade of grass, in every flower, in everything that is alive. In the scheme of nature, everything is connected and correlated with everything else. The groundhog comes out of the earth, and we know it is going to be spring. Birds begin to migrate in a certain direction at a certain time of the year. Nature is a symphony that is silently orchestrated on the ultimate ground of creation. As long as we do not violate the other powers of nature, we can use conscious intent to literally command the powers of nature to fulfil our dreams and desires.

Intention is the real power behind desire because it is desire without attachment to the outcome. Desire in most people is attention with attachment to the outcome. But when we combine intention with detachment, our intent is for the future, while our attention is in the present. Present-moment awareness is powerful, because the future is created by our actions in the present. We cannot take action in the past or in the future. Past and future are born in imagination. Only the present, which is awareness, is real and eternal.

If we practice present-moment awareness, then the imaginary obstacles – which are more than 90 percent of the obstacles – disappear. The remaining obstacles can be transformed into opportunities through on-pointed intention. This means holding our attention to the intended outcome with such unbending purpose that we refuse to allow obstacles to consume our attention, or to dissipate the focused quality of our attention. This is the power of simultaneously practicing focused intention and detachment.

How can you harness the power of intention to fulfil your dreams and desires? You can get result through effort, but if you follow these five steps in the power of intention and desires, your intention will generate its own power:

1) Center yourself in the silent space between thoughts – in the essential state of being.

2) Release your intentions and desires with the expectation that they will bloom when the season is right.

3) Keep your desires to yourself, do not share them with anyone else unless they are closely bonded with you.

4) Relinquish your attachment to the outcome.

5) Let the universe handle the details.

Remember, your true nature is one of pure potentiality. You don't need to look at yourself through the eyes of the world or allow yourself to be influenced by the opinions of others. Remain established in the awareness of your true self. Carry the awareness of your spirit wherever you go, gently release your desires and the universe will orchestrate all the details for you.

To experience the power of intention and desire:

- Make a list of your intentions and desires and look at this list before you go into silence, before you go to sleep at night, and when you wake up in the morning.

- Release your desires into the field of pure potentiality, trusting it to handle all the details for you. Know that when things don't seem to go your way, there is a reason.

- Practice present-moment awareness in all your actions. Refuse to allow obstacles to consume your attention in the present moment.

# Power of Detachment

"I am an enlightened being with infinite compassion. I am detached from the outcome. I am focused on the journey and not the outcome."

The way to acquire anything in the universe is to relinquish our attachment to it. This doesn't mean we give up the intention to create our desire. We don't give up the intention, and we don't give up the desire. We give up our attachment to the outcome. The moment we combine one-pointed intention with detachment to the outcome, we will have what we desire.

Anything we want can be acquired through detachment, because detachment is based on the unquestioning belief in the power of the self. The source of wealth – or of anything in the physical world – is the self, the field of pure potentiality that knows how to manifest everything. All we need to do is nurture our deepest intentions in our heart and go with the flow.

Detachment comes from an inner knowledge that we are a pattern of behavior of a higher intelligence.

When things don't seem to go our way, we can let go of our idea of how things should be. We know that in our limited awareness, we cannot see the synchronistic, harmonious patterns of the universe of which we and our intentions are a part.

Attachment, on the other hand, implies doubt and distrust in nature's intelligence and its infinite organizing power. Attachment is the melodrama of the ego because it is based in fear and insecurity, and this comes from not realizing the power of the self. Those who seek security chase it for a lifetime without ever finding it, because security can never come from material wealth alone. People say, "When I have a million dollars, then I'll be financially independent; then I'll be secure." But it never happens. Attachment to money and security only creates insecurity, no matter how much money we have in the bank.

Attachment to the symbols of wealth – cars, houses, bank notes – creates anxiety because the symbols are transitory. They come and go. When we exchange our self for the symbols of our self, we end up feeling empty inside.

The search for security is actually an attachment to certainty, to the known, and the known is the prison of our past conditioning. Freedom from our past lies in the wisdom of uncertainty. Without uncertainty, life is just a repetition of outworn memories. There's no evolution in that, and when there is no evolution, there is stagnation, entropy and decay.

In ancient philosophical traditions, the solution to this dilemma lay in our willingness to detach from the known, step into the unknown, and surrender our desires to the creative mind that orchestrates the dance of the universe. The unknown is a field of all possibilities, ever fresh, ever new, always open to the creation of new manifestations. This field can orchestrate an infinity of space-time events to bring about the intended outcome. But when our intentions get locked into a rigid mindset, we lose the fluidity, flexibility and creativity inherent in the field. Attachment to a specific outcome freezes our desire into a rigid framework, and this interferes with the whole process of creation. True wealth consciousness is the ability to have anything we want, anytime we want, with the least effort. Detachment is synonymous with wealth consciousness, because with detachment there is freedom to create. How can we create when we're clinging and grasping and full of anxiety? We don't need to have a complete and rigid idea of what we'll be doing next week or next year, because if we get rigidly attached to that idea, then we shut out a whole range of possibilities.

The power of detachment does not interfere with goal setting. We still have the intention of going in a certain direction, but between point A and point B there are infinite possibilities. With uncertainty factored in, we might change direction if we find a higher ideal, or if we find something more exciting. When we experience uncertainty, we're on the right track, and it's the fertile ground of pure creativity and freedom.

How can you apply the power of detachment? Begin by practicing detached involvement. This means whenever you encounter a problem, you stay grounded in the wisdom of uncertainty, while expectantly waiting for a solution to emerge. If you remain detached, you won't feel compelled to force solutions on problems. This enables you to stay alert to opportunities, and what emerges is something powerful and exciting. The state of alert preparedness in the present meets with your goals and intentions and allows you to seize the opportunity within every problem you have in your life.

Every problem is the seed of opportunity for some greater benefit. Once you have this perception, a whole range of possibilities opens up, and this keeps the wonder and excitement alive. Only by practicing detached involvement can you have joy and laughter. Then, wealth is created spontaneously and effortlessly. The word universe means one song. Your every intention or heart's desire is like a melody in nature's symphony. All you have to do is sing your song. In one of his poems Rumi says, ''I want to sing like birds sing, not worrying who listens or what they think.'' If you can sing your song with that attitude, you are participating in the power of detachment, and nothing will be able to stop the force of your intentions. Relinquish your attachment to the known, step into the unknown and experience all the fun, mystery, and magic of what may occur in the field of all possibilities. When your preparedness meets opportunity, a solution will spontaneously appear that benefits you and all those around you.

What is commonly called "good luck" is nothing but preparedness and opportunity coming together. This is the perfect recipe for success, and it is based on the power of detachment.

Practice detached involvement. Stay alert to the opportunity within every problem by letting go of your idea of how things should be.

• Accept uncertainty as an essential part of your experience. In your willingness to accept uncertainty, solutions will appear spontaneously.

• Remain open to all possibilities and enjoy every moment in the journey of your life – all the fun, mystery, and magic in the field of pure potentiality.

# Power of Self - Inquiry

We would all like to know the truth of our existence on this earth. Throughout our life we may seek it by asking questions like:

"Who am I?"

"What am I doing here?"

"Who or what is God?"

"What is the real nature of things?"

"Is what I am experiencing right now really true?"

And so on…

If we ask our questions with feeling and persistence, if we continue to inquire, the answers will come to us sooner or later. How we go about it will determine our rate of progress, and the degree of ease or difficulty we may experience on the road to knowledge. Therefore, a methodology with predictable results can bring some important benefits. We will attempt to deliver a reliable approach to the field of self-enquiry here. It is a novel idea, because the traditional approaches to self-enquiry are often accompanied by much uncertainty, for reasons that will become clear as we move along. Is such uncertainty necessary? Not really. It is only a matter of gaining some education and understanding about the dynamics of human spiritual transformation. With some practical perspective, the journey can be made without pulling the hinges off the divine doorway of our nervous system.

It is a paradox that formal structured approaches to self-enquiry can lead to uncertainty and limited results. We will reveal why this is so. Here, we will take a less structured approach, and not offer a cookbook for self-enquiry. There are plenty of these available already. Instead, we will look at underlying principles, and how we can apply these principles in concert with continuing spiritual progress resulting from a balanced integration of effective Yoga practices.

Through endless enquiry and experimentation over the centuries, humankind has made much progress in determining the truth about our world, and beyond, to the point where applied science has harnessed many principles in nature for our betterment. Some may argue whether all of this progress has been for the better. Nevertheless, the steady expansion of applied knowledge marches on, and we are obliged to make the best of it. Such a progressive approach for the application of steadily accumulating knowledge can also be used in the development and implantation of practical spiritual methods. It is time for that.

In spite of our increasing mastery of the material powers of nature and this small planet we live on, we have done little so far to realize the ultimate truth of who we are and what we are doing here, let alone make such practical use of that exclusive knowledge. Because of this we continue to suffer at the hands of our perceived mortality.

If finding the truth was simply a matter of developing an intellectual understanding, it would be easy – as easy as taking a high school class on physics, including an introduction to the principles of quantum mechanics. With that, we would know that all we see and do in life is playing out in a vast realm of absolute emptiness, with innumerable bits of interacting energy creating the appearance and substance of everything we consider to be our real world.

So, how real is our world if all we see, hear and touch is nothing but energy interacting with itself in vast emptiness? This is a question that cannot be avoided when considering the ultimate consequences of quantum mechanics. Why is there an apparent inconsistency between what physics tells us and the physical world we perceive around us? And how does this inconsistency affect the quality of our life? Can knowing the truth about this alleviate our suffering, as wise people, both ancient and modern, have promised?

We can find out for ourselves through direct experience.

It is a matter of perception. To experience and know more, our perception must be refined. While we cannot perceive radio waves with our normal senses, we have developed the technology to perceive them, and use them for great benefit. Modern technology has opened many doors for us in this way.

Interestingly, the ancient science of Yoga goes quite a lot further than modern science has so far in dealing with the unseen realm of absolute emptiness we are purported to be made of and living in. While modern science relies on devices enabling us to perceive and utilize principles in nature that we cannot see, the field of Yoga relies on the human nervous system to do the same thing and with remarkable results.

While utilizing our own nervous system as the primary instrument for discerning and applying the ultimate truth of life may seem like a new idea, there have been small groups of people doing it for thousands of years. It has been a fragile affair with many disruptions and distortions coming from the forces of chaos, which have been running roughshod over humanity for many centuries. The great religions of the world have spun off and grown from these small groups of spiritual innovators, inevitably mixing truth with politics and the long running struggle of humanity to survive and thrive.

Now we find ourselves in the information age, where knowledge can be more easily distilled, preserved and shared, and it is more difficult for the forces of chaos to have their way. In this way, modern information technology has come to lend a hand to the ancient science of spirit.

Due to rapid rise of knowledge, we have arrived at a turning point, a point where many people around the world can deepen their enquiry about the nature of things. This allows for a shift in perspective to take place. It is possible to include a more penetrating inquiry from the point of view of what is inside us – our radiant inner self.

This has been made possible by the rise of knowledge about integrated spiritual practices in the modern world, with the principles and methods of practical self-inquiry being a part of that.

## Self-inquiry – The Yoga of knowledge

Self-inquiry is not new. It has been a part of Yoga and other systems of spiritual practice for centuries. It has been called jñāna yoga, meaning "union through knowledge." Jñāna means knowledge, and yoga means union of the inner and outer aspects of life. Self-inquiry has also been called the path of discrimination and the path of the intellect. Knowledge of what? Discrimination of what? Intellectual knowledge of what? These are fair questions, and we will attempt to answer them in this book. Jñāna also means wisdom, which points to the deeper level of knowing, a spiritual knowing, which is the end game of self-inquiry, and all of Yoga.

Before we delve into the particulars of self-inquiry and additional Yoga practices upon which its success depends, let's look at the relationship of philosophy and experience, which can help form a framework and basis for a practical approach to self-inquiry.

## Role of Philosophy and Experience

As we begin to think about the true nature of things, it is helpful to have a foundation in the form of an idea or structure. Quantum physics was mentioned for this reason, offering the modern scientific hypothesis of emptiness underlying our physical universe. The ancient philosophical traditions of the east concur with this view, with an additional component added- the presence of consciousness in absolute emptiness which emerges from it. While it may not be possible to verify that the emptiness underlying everything is conscious, we can certainly verify that what manifests from emptiness is conscious, because we are conscious.

Ancient eastern philosophy, and some western philosophies, holds that emptiness is the great self of all, and that all individual selves are but rays emanating from the one great Self, much the way waves dance upon the surface of ocean, only to dissolve and reappear on the surface of the ocean again and again. The waves are ever-changing expressions of the great ocean they dance upon.

Whether the great ocean of emptiness beyond the manifested universe is conscious can be debated. But there can be little debate about whether human beings are conscious. It is this singular fact that underlies the entire field of self-inquiry.

There is a vast theoretical body of knowledge, which can be found in the amply documented philosophies of both the east and the west, plus the experimental component of consciousness which can be found in every human being. Put these two together, and you have the beginnings of self-inquiry.

It is really quite simple. If we can come to know that we are, in fact, the ocean before, during and after we are the wave, then the inquiry is done. Enlightenment is ours. Philosophically, that is called the end of knowledge. In the east, it is called Vedanta- the end of Veda.

But, experientially, it is not so simple. Something more is needed, which is often overlooked by those who hold an uncompromising view of human enlightenment.

If our experience does not fulfill the philosophy, or even the claims of another as their experience, then the inquiry is not complete. While purists may insist that only emptiness exists, it is up to each of us to verify the truth for ourselves. It is for this that the methods of self-inquiry are given.

But it turns out that self-inquiry is very much a moving target, depending on the person who is doing it. Just as certain ideas will resonate with some people and not others, the methods of self-inquiry may resonate with some practitioners and not with others. The reason for this variation is due to the inner condition of each individual's nervous system. The degree of inner purification and opening deep inside has a direct bearing on the degree of consciousness that is available in the person for gaining knowledge of the nature of existence, at least insofar as knowledge can be gained through direct experience within the individual.

The key factor in this is the presence of what we call inner silence, also called pure bliss consciousness, the self, or the witness. It is called the witness because stillness in our awareness is our ground state and, once established, is capable of experiencing all thoughts, perceptions and emotions as objects outside its own unmoving awareness.

The presence of the witness changes the complexion and effectiveness of all self-inquiry methods dramatically and our perception of everyday life as well. What had been a moving target becomes steady, and the very knowledge we have been seeking is what we become. We were that all along, and the witness is that. There is an old saying that what we are seeking is what is doing the seeking. Our inner awareness in the form of the witness is both the goal and the means for attaining it.

The witness can be cultivated in human beings by engaging in self-inquiry. This is its purpose. However, it is very difficult to do it using self-inquiry as the sole means. Ask anyone who has tried without using any other supporting practices.

A much more effective way to cultivate the witness is with daily deep meditation. Once this kind of cultivation occurs on an ongoing basis, then self-inquiry will have the ability to gain some real traction in our lives, and add far-reaching additional benefits that cannot be realized with either deep meditation or self-inquiry alone. When we say "traction," we mean the formation of an intimate relationship between our native consciousness and the object of this world, including our thoughts, feelings and perceptions of the external environment. Our abiding inner witness, combined with self-inquiry, can lead us steadily towards a condition of oneness, beyond the ups and downs of life, even as we are fully engaged and going about our business each day. In this condition, there is no grasping or hanging on.

So, if we are looking for real self-inquiry, we should look beyond the dictums of rigid philosophical systems to the inner workings of our own nervous system. If we do that, we will go beyond ideas to the experience itself. Then the wave will know itself to be the ocean, even as it continues as a wave. Philosophy is therefore a stepping stone to the greatest knowledge of our self.

## The Importance of Practice

There are those who say that practice is not necessary to reach enlightenment. Indeed, the unconditioned state of pure bliss consciousness is beyond all practice. So, they are right in saying that the end state is beyond all practice, and even beyond all experience. When the fluctuations of the mind have been transcended, only the absolute remains. To be in this condition, nothing must be done, and nothing is, at least from the point of view of someone who is in this state on an ongoing basis. But what about everyone else?

The advice not to practice is an extremist view that leads many into confusion, particularly those who have responsibilities in the world. Such advise may be interpreted to mean going on with life as usual (having learnt what?), or rejecting life completely in favor of doing nothing. Either way, there will be a problem.

So, while philosophically the argument not to practice, or do nothing, has appeal, on the practical level it has little relationship to what most people are involved with in their daily life – living or doing. And neither is the advice to not practice particularly helpful to people who are contemplative in their nature, as it will often be interpreted to mean sitting around all day doing nothing.

The question is not so much about whether practice is necessary or not. Practice is not the enemy. Effective practice is about changing the point of view of the practitioner (you and me) in relation to the object of our experience. Consciousness as it is manifested through us has a strong tendency to identify with everything it experiences, mistaking itself to be the object it is observing. This includes the very thoughts and feelings we are having right now.

Once identified with external phenomena, our awareness will say, "I am these thoughts and feelings. I am this body. This is my family, my nation and my world."

Once this occurs, we are on the roller coaster of life – the wheel of birth and death, as the philosophers say. It is very much a dream we create for ourselves.

Those who see through the illusion we have built up within and around ourselves will say, "Just stop identifying with all this. Do nothing. Let it all go."

There is a certain amount of determination a teacher may have in wanting to wake people up to what is.

Lacking more practical means, a teacher may resort to radical advice, which most people will not be able to implement with any degree of reliability.

There are several problems with this radical approach. First, doing nothing. On the level of the mind, the act of letting go is a doing, so it will be a contrary experience for many people. And it is not so easy anyway for most people who are living regular lives. Attempting to take such a radical view with the mind can actually be very destructive to the motivation of the person and seriously disrupt effectiveness in daily life.

So perhaps the conclusion will be to go off to a remote cave where letting go and doing nothing might be more doable. But, alas, there is a problem with this too. Our mind goes with us to the cave, and all that we have been identified with goes with us as well. We take ourselves wherever we go.

The guru who tell us not to practice will tell us to be vigilant in doing nothing. We should practice this in our every waking moment!

It is pretty silly, isn't it? Building a mountain of intention and mental strategies, all for the purpose of doing nothing. The mind can never figure itself out. Only by transcending the mind can we know what the mind and everything else really is.

Once we have come to the recognition that doing nothing is actually doing something, we can begin to take a more practical approach, by doing something that can actually work. And that something is engaging in methods that can gradually dissolve the identification of our awareness with the object of perception. As this identification and the dream in which we inhabit begins to dissolve, the experience will be the rise of inner silence, our consciousness without the encumbrance of identification with the objects of perception, including our own thoughts. This unencumbered awareness, we call the witness.

The witness is not a condition we conjure up in the mind. It cannot be manufactured by the mind. It is a real and permanent presence of our awareness devoid of attachment to the experiences of temporal life. The witness is beyond the mind. Cultivating the witness is the object of self-inquiry and Yoga. Later on, we will learn how the witness also becomes dynamic, illuminating all objects we perceive, from within. Then we are able to do everything without doing anything. But it takes some particular kinds of doing to cultivate this condition of non-doing. This is the outcome of combining a full range of Yoga practices.

While there is a strong tendency for teachers and practitioners to cling to a singular methodology for producing spiritual progress, this is not the most effective approach. It doesn't matter what method is touted as the way. There simply is not a single way that will carry anyone through to the realization we all seek.

The methods of Yoga are not mutually exclusive. They are mutually integrative. Ignoring the full range of Yoga methods that are available in favor of fixation on a single method is a risky proposition at best. Perhaps, there will be some results, and perhaps, there won't. It will depend more on the initial condition of the practitioner than on the method itself. Of course, the initial condition of the practitioner will always determine the initial results. In fact, we could say that those who tend to oversimplify the task of revealing the truth within all of us were naturals from the beginning, needing very little in the way of practice, and what they offer is suitable only for those who are nearly enlightened already.

## And what about the rest of us?

We want more than philosophical platitudes that might tickle a sense of the infinite residing within us. We want to realize it. For this, we have an array of practices that can be integrated in a highly complementary way. Self-inquiry is one of these practices, and it comes into play in a variety of ways in relation to our overall strategy of daily Yoga practices. Let's delve deeper.

# An Approach to Self-Inquiry

While we may often hear that enlightenment is an absolute condition which can be realized immediately by using absolute measures, this is fiction for the vast majority of people. It is an attractive proposition for the mind. We could even say that it is intellectually and emotionally seductive. But it is fiction all the same. Taking such thinking too seriously may lead us to extremist approaches that can delay our spiritual progress rather than enhance it.

There is a middle way.

As soon as we come to the realization that enlightenment is a journey rather than an instant event, we will be open to infinite possibilities, and many doors will begin to open. If we remain open, we will find that an integration of methods can bring us to the realization that we have been seeking, and with far less effort. Ironically, the multifold track is the track of least doing, and certainly the one of least angst.

## Can it be that simple?

The approach to self-inquiry is to integrate it naturally into our life as part of our general routine. In part, self-inquiry is what we have the option to do as we go about our normal daily life, between our twice-daily sittings of structured practices. Self-inquiry of this kind is less structured and highly individualistic. It may draw on different teachings at different times. However, there are several levels of application in self-inquiry which are essential to understand, mainly so we can stay in synchronization with our own spiritual progress. It is important to understand where we are in relation to our practice, and pace our practice to accommodate the changes that are occurring within us. This applies to self-inquiry as much as with any other practice we are utilizing. So, we will be systematic in our approach here, but not issue cookbook instructions for self-inquiry. Our practice will be determined by our own inner inclination and the application of sound principles. It is the most progressive and safe approach to spiritual development, assuming we are working with the underlying principles of human spiritual transformation and integrating time-tested techniques.

We will be doing many things in order to be doing nothing in the stillness of our inner awareness.

The primary aim of self-inquiry is to remain established in the unconditioned inner silence that resides within all of us – the experiencer, the witness to all thoughts, feelings and perceptions of the body and external phenomena.

Self-inquiry seeks to dissolve the identification of awareness with all of these perceptions. The traditional wisdom holds that the abiding presence of the witness (undifferentiated consciousness) will be the effect of self-inquiry. It can be, and this is the aim of all who pursue self-inquiry as a stand-alone path. All the various strategies (mental algorithms) of self-inquiry are oriented towards this realization.

However, it is also true that the presence of the witness is the cause of self-inquiry. When the witness is present, a natural inclination towards self-inquiry becomes self-evident, for then the innate condition of the practitioner as the witness becomes the answer to every inquiry – the eternal illness that does nothing even as life carries on in all of its diversity. Once the witness is present, self-inquiry becomes more or less automatic. The witness is both the fuel and the destination of self-inquiry.

In this approach, we seek to cultivate the witness first by the most effective means at our disposal.

We begin by establishing a practice of daily deep meditation. In doing so, we insure the fruition of all we undertake in self-inquiry, and our permanent realization of the truth.

## Deep Meditation and the inner witness

Deep meditation is a specific practice that is designed to cultivate inner silence, which is the witness, regarded to be a prerequisite for self-inquiry in the current approach.

Deep meditation is a very simple practice, and it is very powerful. It is so powerful that it only needs to be practiced for 15-20 minutes twice daily. That is more than enough to set us on the road of cultivating the witness, and self-inquiry grows naturally out of that.

This style of meditation involves the use of a mantra, and repeatedly refining it to stillness with a specific procedure. The mantra used is I AM, and the procedure involves mental repetition of the mantra without regard to meaning. Deep meditation is not an inquiry into the meaning of I AM. It is systematically transcending the vibration of I AM in the mind to reach stillness. In this way, stillness is cultivated in the mind, not only during deep meditation, but more importantly, during the time we are not meditating while undertaking daily activities. Then, inner silence comes to be known as a witnessing quality in our life, which open up the possibility for more effective self-inquiry. When we have inner silence, self-inquiry is the natural result, because we will come to know our thoughts and feelings to be objects of perception, rather than who we are. It becomes evident that we are the witness, and we can engage with everything else without the bondage of the identification of awareness with experience of life.

Becoming the witness also leads to the end of suffering, for suffering ceases when awareness is no longer identified with pain. Pain will still be there as before, along with all the rest of life's experiences, but suffering will not be there. Suffering is the identification of the mind with pain, discomfort and the failure of desires to be fulfilled. When we have become the witness, we will still experience all of these things on the surface, but will not suffer within ourselves. Self-inquiry has a key role to play in our coming to the realization that the witness, who we are, does not suffer. Indeed, self-inquiry is an ideal practice for completing the journey of our witness-self becoming free of the last traces of the identification of our awareness with the temporal aspects of life.

Does it mean we leave life, cease to be engaged or interested in what is going on around us? No, it does not mean that. It is quite to the contrary. The cultivation of inner silence via deep meditation enhances positive qualities within us – the flowering of compassion, love, and the energy to engage in the world of evolutionary ways. This may seem in contrast to the classical view of self-inquiry, which may exhort us to drop all attachments in the world. With the rise of the witness, that is what happens. We cease to be identified with the occurrences that take place in time and space, while at the same time we overflow with outpouring love in the very realm we have transcended. We can let go of the world even as we are illuminating it naturally from within. Our actions will tell the tale, for we will be doing much more for others, even as we are doing less inside. This is the power of the witness when cultivated into full presence within the individual.

Inner silence is at the heart of all of Yoga, and at the heart of all systems of spiritual knowledge and unfoldment. Without inner silence, there would be no systems of spiritual development. Inner silence is the spirit within us and all things.

All spiritual paths are about revealing our "I", and becoming it in its native unconditioned state. All spiritual tracks are for answering the question "who am I"? and consciously becoming That. Our nervous system has the ability to reveal that reality within us, and more. This is why we call the human nervous system the doorway to the infinite.

With direct experience through deep meditation, self-inquiry, and other integrated practices, we can go from the philosophy/theory of inner silence to the reality of it. The leap from theory to reality is found in the ways that our nervous system manifests different forms of awareness. The witness alive in us is known to be that ever-awake sense of "I" during waking, dreaming and deep sleep stages of awareness. Inner silence is a state distinctly different from the other three stages mentioned above. In deep meditation, it is blissful awareness without any objects. Once cultivated as distinct, the witness will be there underlying all objects as well – our thoughts, feelings and external experiences.

The difference between inner silence and the temporal states of consciousness is that inner silence is unchanging and can be cultivated in the nervous system as an unending presence superimposed under, in, and through the other three stages of consciousness.

With daily deep meditation, inner silence begins as inner peace and an awareness of a silent quality coexisting with and within the objects of our perception in daily living. This happens with external observations through the senses, and with our thoughts and feelings. We see them as the objects that they are, occurring external to our unconditioned inner silent awareness. With sustained practice of daily deep meditation and the integration of additional practices that are available, inner silence grows and becomes the movie screen upon which all our experiences are projected. We become the movie screen – the infinite movie screen of life. It is what we are. It is our essential nature.

Inner silence is the space between our thoughts. It is the gap we sometimes experience as we pass from one thought to another, and from one state of consciousness to another. When the music stops for an instant, we are left with inner silence, our true self.

Keep in mind that inner silence is not on the level of the curious mind or the intellect. It is beyond all thinking and philosophy. In that sense, the call to do nothing is valid. In order to do that we must do something.

Daily practices exist for purifying and opening our nervous system – a dramatic expansion of the function of our neurobiology, leading to true knowledge of what is. So, cultivating inner silence directly through daily deep meditation has far-reaching implications in our approach to self-inquiry, and in the quality of our life – a life that can be lived in fulfillment, without suffering.

## Self-inquiry – From inspiration to Realization

Next to devotion, which is the cornerstone of all the spiritual traditions of the world, self-inquiry is the most common spiritual technique on the earth. In fact, it isn't even considered a spiritual technique by many who engage in it. It is simply on ongoing inquiry for truth.

As little children, it is likely we have asked, "who am I?" and "why I am here?". The way in which we have answered these questions in the past have determined to a large degree what we have done with our lives up until now. And if we have not been too hardened by life, we are likely still asking these questions. We are aired for it. We simply must know the truth about life. It is an endless search for purpose and meaning.

Perhaps, at some point we read or heard that life is unbounded and that human beings can experience this unbounded nature of life, and became more curious about such a life. Somehow it rang true, and we were inspired. Perhaps we have been inspired ever since.

It is from there that we began our quest for knowledge in earnest, only to find that the mind alone, while very good for entertaining ideas, even one so grand as enlightenment, will leave us either stuck in frustration or lost in a labyrinth of endless streams of thought. Even the thought of letting go can create more mental structures and inertia.

The more we think about it, the more frustrating it can become. The mind just isn't the place to solve the riddle of enlightenment. The key is to go beyond the mind. We don't have to kill our mind or our thoughts to do this. We just need to find our center in the witness, which is beyond the mind and easily favor that. Then the mind becomes our friend again. The mind makes a poor master, but a very good servant. Our goal is not to get rid of the mind or thinking. The goal is to dissolve the identification of our mind as our self, our ego, to wake up from the dream that we have been living in. It is not the destruction of the ego or the mind. Only a shift to become identified as the great blank screen behind the grand movie of our life – the witness.

So, it is very important what we do with the inspiration that our initial self-inquiry may bring us. If we use the inspiration to propel us into sound methods for transcending the mind to stillness, then we will find the possibility to move from inspiration to transformation.

The idealist touting a philosophical approach will say that there is no transformation to be had, for everything is as it should be right now. We must only realize it in the now. But that realization is also a transformation, and it cannot occur until our perception opens up enough that we are able to see what is. Without the witness, it will not happen.

It is possible to spend many years in self-inquiry, pondering the truth behind things and studying the words of those who know over and over again. Such writings are plentiful, easily accessed these days, and can be very inspiring. Yet, no matter how many times we read these words, or engage in the logic of particular modes of self-inquiry, we may feel quite distant from what the words and ideas are attempting to convey. The reason is because we can only know within ourselves, and for that, the perception of our own inner silence as our self must be opened. We need the witness.

Then, when we read the words of the wise, they will resonate more each time. It will not be the words that change us. It will be we who have changed, and we will see more truth in all expressions of knowledge as we continue to open to our native awareness inside.

Self-inquiry itself is not a very effective way to cultivate the witness. It is the underlying principle of meditation that cultivates the witness – always. To some extent self-inquiry can aid us in dissolving the objects of the mind, it will cultivate the witness. In doing so, it will be utilizing the principle of meditation – gradually dissolving the identification of our awareness with objects to become increasingly identified with the subject, which is the witness. Self-inquiry is not necessarily the most efficient kind of meditation, but it can be a kind of meditation all the same.

The important thing about our early days of self-inquiry, and our budding desire for truth, is that we transform the inspiration gained into useful measures that will unfold the witness within us. If we do that, then we will find ourselves coming back to self-inquiry later on with much more clarity than we had in the beginning. So, the approach that is suggested here is to inquire, be inspired, unfold the witness in daily deep meditation, and then inquire some more when the urge arises naturally from within us, as it surely will. This is an approach that is self-sustaining and will lead to much progress, peace and joy in life.

It is the journey from inspiration to realization, and what we do in-between will make all the difference.

## Relational and Non-Relational self-inquiry

In its purest form, self-inquiry takes the position that nothing exists. There is only I AM. In fact, in pure self-inquiry, there is no "I," for "I" must utilize a vehicle of expression. And AM does not exist either. The self-awareness of AM cannot be verified, except as a sense of being described after the fact. The description of the AM is only that, a description. The same can be said of the witness, even if we self-identify with it at all times. The witness is awareness independent of all objects. Yet, the witness does coexist with objects, as anyone who engages in daily deep meditation for a while knows. So, we can try and describe it, even though it is who we are beyond all descriptions. It is a riddle.

The coexistence of the witness with objects is not generally accepted by those engaged in the most uncompromising forms of self-inquiry, even as they engage with objects and walk about doing daily activities ranging from the mundane to the complex. Their assertion is that there are no objects. In uncompromising approaches to self-inquiry, we are instructed to let life go and reside in that which is behind the illusion. We are told, "Be the blank screen behind the movie."

It is all well and good. It is the truth. We are That and all objects are projections within That. However, this kind of thinking will only be thinking if there is no abiding witness present while such concepts are being entertained. And therein lies the problem, a power in the impeccable logic of pure uncompromising self-inquiry.

The premise is that if one engages in this kind of thinking for long enough, then eventually the letting go that results will lead to realization, and cognition of

That which is beyond the play occurring in time and space, which is presumed to have no reality whatsoever. This "realization" can be instant. It is said so.

There is an inconsistency in this approach. Not for everyone, but for a large percentage of the population. The problem is that for those who are yet to cultivate abiding inner silence (the witness) this kind of self-inquiry will be largely intellectual. That which is being sought in letting go is also a thought object in the mind. So, it is thoughts about thoughts. The mind playing with the mind. It can go on for a very long time.

This kind of self-inquiry can lead to much trouble in life – an attitude of meaninglessness and a loss of motivation to engage in living. The very act of affirming non-duality (un-manifest oneness) and the non-existence of duality (oneness plus diversity) can lead to a sense of hopelessness if one is not experiencing at least a smidgen of the thing itself, the witness.

It is like asking a bird who is yet to grow wings to jump off the top of the building. The bird with fully developed and functioning wings will keep saying to the one with undeveloped wings, "Come on you can do it. Just jump. Don't worry about the wings."

Does this make any sense? The wings have to come first. Then we can fly.

It is time to face up to the fact that one method of self-inquiry does not apply to all. Cookbook self-inquiry in the form of mental algorithms and formula thinking does not work for everyone.

Rather, self-inquiry is a continuum that is tied to the level of inner silence we are experiencing as a known presence within us. It is the witness. That is the real thing. That is the blank screen behind the movie of life. When we engage in self-inquiry from that position, then we will have a relationship between consciousness (our witness) and the idea. Then, there can be an intimate cognition in silence of the reality conveyed by the idea. This is knowledge.

On the other hand, if we identify largely with our thoughts, and perceive these to be our self, then the idea of our thoughts will be interacting with the idea of our self– two ideas interacting with each other. Castles in the air. In this case, there is no intimate relationship between consciousness and the idea. It is all happening in the mind.

It is important to understand these two situations, and how a natural shift will occur as we, as the witness, move into true relationship with our thoughts, feelings, and perceptions of the surroundings, leading to direct cognition of who and what we are. If we develop clarity about what the maneuvering of our mind is and what our true presence is, then we will find ourselves going beyond all objects, including all thoughts. We will be going beyond the mental processes of self-inquiry as well, which is the only true self-inquiry – that which dissolves thinking immediately with the first question, and that which inhabits all answers of stillness. Of course, this is made possible by cultivating the witness in daily deep meditation.

In order to better gauge where we are, it can be helpful to designate parameters to describe where we may be in our efforts to engage in self-inquiry. Such designations would not be necessary if all who entered into self-inquiry were coming from the same place – the point of view of the inner witness. However, this is not the case, so making some distinctions can be helpful.

The truth is that much of the self-inquiry that goes on these days is non-relational (meaning, not progressive) and often counterproductive to spiritual progress, because it adds layers of mental baggage without much cultivation of our native awareness. Ironically, effective practices which do cultivate the witness may be shunned in favor of such a rigid approach, which do not cultivate a relationship between the objects of perception and the witness. So much of self-inquiry today is like this, and many find themselves beating their head against a wall. It isn't necessary!

On the other hand, for the few who have had abiding inner silence since an early age, there will almost always be a relationship between ideas and infinite awareness. Self-inquiry in this case is relational. These are the spontaneously awakened souls who dazzle us with their insight and who are often idolized and imitated. There is an air of exclusivity about them, which can unintentionally lead to a have or have not mentality.

Enlightenment is not an exclusive condition reserved for the few, and the rest of us are not doomed to imitate the instruction to "just be." No. With the addition of deep meditation and other practices that promote the cultivation of the witness, and much more, self-inquiry can be relational and the direct cognition of life as a dance of endless joy in emptiness. It is there for everyone.

By relational self-inquiry, we mean a progressive and intimate relationship between ideas and our inner consciousness. When our thoughts are naturally witnessed as objects, something happens. A joining occurs, and the idea dissolves along with its meaning in stillness. Then, we are able to know the truth of it.

For example, if we ask the question, "Who am I?" and let go into our stillness, the answer will be there, not as an idea, but as part of us in presence. We will know who we are beyond the surroundings, our body, thoughts and feelings. If we have been cultivating inner silence in daily deep meditation, the answer will be there to an increasing degree over time, until eventually all that we have known to be other will be dancing on our field of awareness like waves in the unmoving depths of the ocean.

On the other hand, if we go about mentally chanting, "Who am I? Who am I? Who am I?" pounding the idea away without any significant stillness or presence of the witness, without any letting go, this will be non-relational self-inquiry. It can lead to a lot of frustration, and real headaches. Much better to get behind all that by developing our inner quality of stillness, which we can then let go into easily when engaged in self-inquiry.

In our daily activities and relationships, we may be inclined to inquire about the nature of the experiences and interactions we encounter. If someone becomes angry with us, and we find ourselves responding in kind, we may inquire, "Is my rising anger based in truth?" and then let it go into stillness. If we are abiding in the witness, the answer will be there. We will know that our negative reactions are rooted in our identification with the body-mind, which we have falsely regarded as our self. As we become identified with the anger of another, we may be inclined to mirror that. But is that the truth? Can't we just as easily mirror the anger of another with a loving reply? What have we got to lose but the anger itself? The abiding witness gives us the ability to make that choice, where before the witness we could only react to negative energy in kind. The witness puts us in the position of having a choice, and when we have that choice, we have the option to take the high road.

Life operates on knee-jerks, on habits and dramatic stories that have been deeply ingrained in us for a long time. We draw our conclusions about every situation in life based on these habits. It is like we are the hero/heroine in our drama and everyone else is the potential enemy. It doesn't have to be this way. As we begin to see the world and ourselves from the perspective of our own inner silence, we will also see that we can change our reactions to things. We will be compelled to do so, because the truth rising within us does not mesh with the untrue habit we have been unintentionally expressing in so many ways. So, we begin to make different choices about how we act, based on what we are actually seeing.

Oddly, if we project this divine process of choosing beyond where we are in stillness in the present, there will be strain. As soon as we do that, we will find ourselves slipping into non-relational self-inquiry, building more mental structures, often in ways we may not even recognize. Relationship is letting go. Non-relationship is hanging on, including on to letting go!

It is the difference between theory and practice. Theory is thinking about doing, and practice is the doing itself. So much of self-inquiry out there is only about theory, about philosophy. Real self-inquiry is about practice, about the thing itself, which is engaging as the witness.

Why bother with all this relational and non-relational mumbo-jumbo? It is suggested not to bother with it much. We don't want to be adding too much mental baggage. Just recognize that self-inquiry is not about doing, projecting or protecting. It is about going beyond the machinations of the mind with simple questions and automatic answers that rise in stillness – easily favoring the stillness within. Our ability to do this is directly related to the degree of inner silence we have present. So be sure to take care of the business of cultivating inner silence before engaging in self-inquiry. Then you will be flying on the wings of the witness.

# Constitution of Mind

Mind itself is the individual, only that which is done by the mind is regarded as done and not that which is done by the body. The body is activated by the mind just as a tree is shaken by the wind.

Contrary to those who claim man is born with *tabula rasa* - a blank slate (in the mind), Vedanta teaches that the mind is filled with many influences from the past. The mind is the only thing that accompanies the soul from the previous birth. We don›t bring our former body, hair, eye color, physique or gender from the past. We bring attachments, we bring unfulfilled desires and we often bring the last thoughts, the last state of mind from our previous body with us. We also bring with us a selection from the store of past karmas - called *prarabdha* karma - along with the mind into the new fetus which emerges from the womb.

Other influences on the mind include what is sometimes called the family karmic pool - the karmas that are passed down from previous generations.

There are also other influences that shape and form the mind: the learning environment, the influence of teachers, the (sometimes) deleterious influence of peers, along with that of society and culture. Einstein once said, "If you want to know who a man is, show me his friends." It is an oft repeated axiom that "culture shapes mind" and the impact of culture on mind is all-encompassing. We know about culture shock when people settle in a new environment with a different language, customs and values.

The mind-body complex is made up of very fine instruments of perception (*jnanendriayas*) and action (*karmendriyas*). There is also the *antarkaranas*, the interior instruments of awareness and decision making. These comprise the mind (which is wavering in nature), the *buddhi* (or intellect) when the mind is concerned with thoughts, the *Chitta* - recollection and consciousness when the mind is concerned with self-inquiry and understanding, and *ahamkara* - the ego with its sense of I, Me, Mine. The mind is the key to the nobility of the human; turn the key to the world, the *ahamkara* takes over, and turns the mind to self-inquiry and understanding rules the roost.

When we come to look at the strengths of mind - evidenced by thoughts, words and action - we assess the character of a person. We can say a person has a strong character and is self-reliant. We can observe that another person has weak character and follows others without thinking for themselves. Strength of character rests on knowledge, skill, balance, insight and identity. These are the fine instruments of the mind that require diligence, practice and constant self-awareness. Cultivation of these skills is simply the fruit of delayed gratification, self-control, self-discipline and self-respect. Psychologists teach that those who practice delaying of gratification - in most instances - achieve the goals they set for themselves. Hence, we see that the mind and its strengths - or weaknesses - are all important in terms of understanding our character, understanding ourselves and crafting a path through life with our own gifts, skills and unique contributions to the game called life.

To use a metaphor, the mind is like a little child. We have to raise the child, train them not to do harmful things and to be safe and careful. We have to train the little child and teach the child good habits, and repetition reinforces good habits. We teach the little child right from wrong, truth from lies, good from bad. We inculcate good habits and elicit the values within. We raise the little child, train the child to become wiser and wiser and caress the child onto good ways. We make the child aware that all objects that are 'seen' are just products of their own illusion, remove all fears and foibles, and focus attention steadily on one goal only, '*Doing the Truth*'.

The unregulated mind, on the other hand, will strip away the carefully placed boundaries within the mind with discontent and desire. The unregulated mind will tell the mind that 'the grass is greener on the other side' and push the mind to disobey the inner voice of truth within and obtain the object of desire at any cost. The unregulated mind hates to follow dharma - righteousness - for righteousness is simply a barrier on the journey to fulfilment of desire. The unregulated mind - shadow planet of smoke and haze - fans the fires of desire and the smokescreen produced wafts away all steadiness and balance. As an example, you might think of Toad of Toad Hall, totally infatuated with the auto-mobile. Toad desires an auto-mobile at any cost, re-enacts the sights, sounds, smells, touch and feel of the auto-mobile and wastes time in airy reminisces of the same. Infatuation, in other words. The unregulated mind makes the mind infatuated with the object of desire.

## *How everything can be lost*

The unregulated mind fosters and multiplies intense periods of inactivity and inaction. Intense, due to the time filled with desire. Time that is not filled with beneficial activity leads to inactivity, idleness. This can lead to loss of capacity to discriminate right from wrong. Idleness is a trap. It can lead to a loss of discrimination. Idleness generates desire, desire comes up against frustration, and unregulated mind is a giver of persistent frustration. Desire produces an expectation that it be fulfilled, and disappointment when it is not fulfilled. Disappointment leads to anger, which then leads to a state of mind called *sammoha*, stupefaction of the mind. The mind loses its inner connection to the instruments of wisdom (called *jnanendriayas*) and is filled with aberrations. It can no longer connect to the intellect and receive guidance. Memory loss of right from wrong along the guidance of the voice of conscience are lost. The intellect is destroyed. Then everything is lost. We lose our true humanness in the unbridled pursuit of desire. We have to examine how we use time, and how misuse of time can disconnect us from the voice of the intellect within.

*We never deal forcibly with the mind. It will yield easily to tenderness and patient training. Correct its waywardness by means of the attitude of renunciation. Destroy its ignorance by means of instruction in the knowledge of the soul. Strengthen the interest by which it is already endowed toward the realization of God. Let the mind give up the attraction towards the evanescent and the false mirages created by fancy and fantasy. Turn its face inwards, away from the external world. By these methods, concentration can be firmly established.*

The Vedas talk about *nasryeoniyamam vina*, there can be no progress without adherence to discipline. Taking our metaphor earlier of the mind being like a little child whom we guide along the right paths with tenderness and patient training, this is the discipline we offer the child in order to progress through life. Unregulated mind is undisciplined and can cloud two very important functions of the intellect: detachment and discrimination, *vairagya* and *viveka*.

According to Vedanta, detachment (*vairagya*) is not abandoning one's family and living in the forest. One is required to live in society and perform one's duties while keeping the mind free from desires and attachments. The mind is like a piece of cloth, the desires are like the strands of thread. To lighten the mind through the journey of life, we remove the desires one by one, day by day.

Discrimination (*viveka*) is the capacity to recognize the nature of the objective world. Discrimination teaches you how to choose who and what you will have in your life. It teaches you the relative importance of objects and ideals. Discrimination as part of the intellect is the faculty of reason. Where our reason is thwarted or clouded, we will not be making sensible decisions in line with our essential character. The journey of life will go off the rails. We lose the direction, we do not know the path, and we cannot reach the goal.

- Unregulated mind is ambition over-leaping itself (as Shakespeare wrote) and ignoring the rules and boundaries of propriety and behavior.

- Regulated mind is awareness of the goals of life, and the practice of dharma - righteousness in behavior, speech and thought.

- Unregulated mind is the great fraud dissatisfied with the state of affairs and seeks any means to raise their status higher.

- Regulated mind is steadiness in pursuit of learning, application of learning to *artha* - how we earn our wealth and the observance of proper boundaries.

- Unregulated mind hates boundaries and will seek any way to bend the rules including outright fraud (*charakaraka*), cheating and deceit.

- Regulated mind enjoys the good things of life - in fee simple or large - whatever is possible - and sails down the middle of the river of life, careful of the bunds.

We have used the metaphor of a little child. We lead the child along with the caresses of love, and we guide the child along the right path in life. The same applies to our mind, we establish a strong foundation for good character, integrity, and behavior which reflects the values within. We develop discrimination and detachment, we cultivate delay of gratification and follow our goals in life. Regulated mind leads to largesse, expansion. We have a situation where unregulated mind can multiply desires, needs and wants, and as *charakaraka*, dispositor of fraud and obtaining the objects of desire any-which-way, then we can understand that we need to find balance within and rest upon the tried and true values that others have taught us and trust those who inspire us with their example. We understand the need to exercise caution and vigilance over expansive desires and needs, resorting to the familiar inner paths of our discrimination and detachment. We reiterate, the *tried and true paths within*, for unregulated mind that clouds the intellect.

There are many schools of self-inquiry, embodying a variety of systems of practice. Each may emphasize a particular angle, with its own philosophy, terminology and mental algorithms.

The methods can vary widely, from prescribing complete conscious engagement (mindfulness) in the minutest detail of life, to letting go of life altogether. Whatever the teaching may be, it will always reflect the experience of the particular teacher who is transmitting the knowledge. There will be a bias, and the teaching may or may not resonate with all students who come to study that approach. When a student does not get it, it is usually regarded to be the shortcoming of the student, not the teaching itself, which is often held as immutable.

Well, perhaps the end result is immutable, the realization of the eternal within the student. But if the teaching does not help open the door, it can only be the teaching that is failing, not the student. This is a common problem with teachings that are fixed, held high up on a pedestal, and not adaptable for students at many different levels of readiness.

Of what use are such teachings to the masses in modern times? They are from a past era when only the few were regarded to be worthy of spiritual knowledge. In fact, only those who were near enlightenment already were capable of gaining much from such teachings. And those few likely would have finished the task of human spiritual transformation, regardless.

Times are changing. Now, it is time for spiritual teachings to serve the people, instead of the other way around. And in order to do so, the teachings must be open, flexible and most importantly, effective. To be effective, such teachings must be capable of addressing every student at every level of readiness. If the student has the desire to grow and is willing to make a commitment of time and some discipline, then the teaching must be able to deliver viable means, or it will be in need of some improvement. This is okay. If teachings are flexible, they will learn to serve the people where they are and evolve as the people evolve.

Self-inquiry is particularly tricky in terms of application for different levels of students. In our case, we will begin with daily deep meditation, which will cultivate inner silence in everyone. Additional methods of Yoga will be added as appropriate. A foundational knowledge of self-inquiry will also be necessary.

First, it is good to know that in our essential nature we are unbounded pure bliss consciousness, and all we are doing through practice is unfolding what we already are in our daily life. It is also good to know that this will lead to many practical benefits. So, it is a worthwhile endeavor to be on the track.

Next, it is also good to know that there is a natural progression in our spiritual unfoldment which occurs over time, except in the rare cases of people who are born near enlightenment. In spite of what we may have heard, enlightenment is not an overnight event for most people. There is no getting around this, because each of us must go through a process of inner purification and opening, and it takes time, even with the best of teachings. Along the way, there are grades and stages and the journey never ends, even for those who are very advanced. Perhaps, especially for them, because they become much more aware of the wider need for inculcating inner silence in the community, world and beyond, they find themselves on the front line of that great endeavor. We all help as we can, and the enlightened can help so much more. The more we can do, the more we will be called to do.

For the individual, there is a progression of integrated practices that is mapped out step-by-step in Vedanta writing, for cultivating the necessary purification and opening. For self-inquiry, there is a progression as well. Of course, it is not necessary for everyone to go through a progression of self-inquiry methods. One might not even be using structured self-inquiry methods at all, and still be going through the process of self-inquiry based on the natural emergence of inner silence and increasingly clear perceptions of self in relation to the object of experience. Regardless of structured self-inquiry methods, or the lack of them, some recognizable stages will evolve, and it can save time and some confusion to be aware of these, particularly for those who have a tendency to try and run to the end before covering the beginning or the middle. The beginning and the middle can be just as fulfilling as the end if we are aware of where we are on our path. It does not have to be so mysterious. With some basic knowledge, we will do much better, and not be exposed so much to the hazards of taking blind leaps.

Assuming one is engaged in daily deep meditation, here are the five stages of mind that self-inquiry may play itself upon as we move along in our development:

1. Pre-witnessing – information and intellectual assessments about truth provide inspiration, and a tendency to build mental castles in the air,

ideas reacting with ideas, which is non-relational self-inquiry. So, we do what is necessary to cultivate the witness.

2. Witnessing – perceiving the world, our thoughts and feelings as objects separate from self. It is the beginning of relational self-inquiry, chosen or not.

3. Discrimination – the reversal of identification by logical choices based on direct perception rooted in stillness. This more advanced relational self-inquiry which is able to discern the real from the unreal.

4. Dispassion – rise of the condition of no judgement and no attachment. The process of self-inquiry becoming automatic to the point of all objects and self-inquiry itself being constantly dissolved in the witness.

5. Merging of subject and object – "I am That. You are That. All this is That." Ongoing outpouring divine love, service to others and unity.

While progress on the road to enlightenment may be erratic, difficult or non-existent when engaged in self-inquiry as a stand-alone approach, it is quite a different story when self-inquiry is used in combination with a track based on an integration of tried and true Yoga methods.

The cultivation of inner silence (the witness) in deep meditation assures that our perception will be expanding from within over time, and this provides for an increasingly fertile field for the process of self-inquiry to occur.

The steady emergence of inner silence with practices is the dynamic behind the progression of self-inquiry from non-relational to relational, until the experiencer and the experience have merged to become the one.

## *Pre-witnessing*

How meaningful is self-inquiry of the absolute kind when we are still in the pre-witnessing stage of mind? This is when all things are still considered primarily on the level of thinking and logic. In this state, what does it mean to us when we hear, "All this you see here in the world is illusion, and you are the reality behind it."

We might have some inspiration. A desire may be kindled in us to know more. Hopefully. But the more we think about it, the more layers we will create around that essential desire to know the truth. How many times will we have to repeat the question "Who am I"? before we will have a glimmer of who and what we really are? And how many books will we have to read? This is why we call pre-witnessing the stage of inspiration and building castles in the air. Not much more than this can happen until we move to the next stage. With suitable inspiration, we will be compelled to take action beyond pounding the idea against the infinite with our tiny brain!

Once we are inspired to uncover the truth, it is important to take action. Self-inquiry purists will say, "Take no action. Do nothing. Just be!" Well, we can attempt to do that for a very long time in the pre-witnessing mode. No doubt we can develop some witness quality by working on just being for a long time. But there is a much faster away.

If we commit to action using all the tools that are available to us, we can travel very quickly along the road of realization to our innermost self. With deep meditation and a full battery of supporting practices we will surely move into the witnessing stage.

## *Witnessing*

The witnessing stage is a whole new ball game. It should be pointed out that there is witnessing. There is a continuum of development as witnessing emerges. It begins as a passive inner condition perceived as a separation from the events going on around us, often noticed first during the occurrence of dynamic events. Everyone has had the experience of time standing still when a dynamic event occurs, like a car crash, explosion or another sudden change in our physical environment. When the witness begins to emerge, ordinary events are increasingly experienced in this way as well. As witnessing continues to advance, our body, thoughts and feelings become objects of perception that are separate from our sense of self, our witness. This is an important development.

Before the witness has developed to the point where our thoughts and feelings become objects of perception, self-inquiry will mostly be non-relational, meaning not fully connected with who we are – pure consciousness. The dawn of the witness sets the stage for real self-inquiry, and an ongoing change in our life experience, for this is when the process can move beyond ideas to the direct experience. And the direct experience is beyond all experience. In the initial witness condition, we are experiencing, but we are not the experience. We are beyond it, seeing from the point of view of separate pure awareness.

There are few more steps after the emergence of the witness that we must go through. It is not enough to be strongly established in the inner silence, seeing the changing world as separate from ourselves. We must do something with it to move it forward. Evolution compels us to do so. With a little nudging, it happens naturally enough. This is where self-inquiry can have its greatest impact on us, in our overall track to enlightenment, because we are able to make conscious choices based in our stillness. We see our thoughts, feelings and perceptions of the world for what they are, without entirely identifying with them. We are then able to engage in a way that is liberating rather than binding, both for ourselves and for others.

## Discrimination

When we think of discrimination, the normal interpretation is that we choose between this or that thing – choose between this or that idea. Non-rational self-inquiry is like that, choosing between things, ideas, and ways in which we imagine life. This kind of discrimination goes nowhere fast, and may go nowhere for a long time. Even choosing not to think is a gigantic task when undertaken non-rationally, without the witness present to support our endeavor.

With the rising presence of witness, the entire dynamic of self-inquiry changes. Then we are choosing between that which is object (things, ideas, emotions) and that which is subject (witness, self). And that kind of choosing is not doing at all. It is a letting go.

We all know what we want. We want to know the truth. We want to be happy. We want to be free. Since childhood we have been told that the truth will set us free from the burdens of this life. So, we want That.

As the witness becomes more and more abiding and we come to know ourselves as That, unshaken and separate from all of our experiences, including our own thoughts, then we are finally in the position to make choices that will unwind the habitual identification with experiences and the dream we have been in up until now.

It is a new perspective from which we can clearly see what is real and what is not. At the same time, it is both as profound and as simple as directly perceiving what is eternal and what is not. And we can discriminate accordingly, making logical choices that are grounded in stillness, unwinding the lingering habit of the mind to identify itself with the objects of experience, both outside and inside us.

In the language of Yoga, it is called *neti neti*, which means not this and not this. When the witness is sufficiently present for relational self-inquiry to occur in the form of discrimination, then *neti neti* becomes a reality. We directly perceive what is true and what is not and we can easily choose. Before this stage, *neti neti* is an exercise of the intellect, and can be as ineffective and exhausting as any other non-relational self-inquiry. We will know the witness is dawning in earnest when discrimination becomes easier. It is a telltale sign.

A certain excitement comes with the realization that we have arrived at the point of being able to choose with certainty that which is real over that which is not. There can even be an enthusiasm to the exclusion of all else, and we have to guard against throwing out the practices that have brought us to this point. There can be a strong tendency to plant our flag on the notion that we are That, and fixating on the idea that all we have to do from then on is hang on to That.

If this happens, it can be slipping into non-relational self-inquiry again. It can happen to advanced practitioners. It is much better if we continue with the practices that brought us to this point and strengthen the presence of the witness beyond any conviction that we have attained anything. Even the most advanced practitioners must guard against falling into non-relational self-enquiry.

Certainly, we can take giant leaps towards realization when our ability has arisen to clearly discriminate between objects (external and internal) and the subject (the witness – our self). It is the prime time for self-inquiry. But it will not be only thing going on, assuming we have ben wise and continue with our daily routine of Yoga practices. All methods combined will assure our rapid progress.

Self-inquiry is useful, but it cannot be trusted to operate alone. Certainly not at the discrimination stage, or at any prior stage.

There will come a time when discrimination begins to give way to something else. It is the letting go of the need to make choices anymore. The subject (witness) becomes so well established that choices no longer need to be made. We just are and we can allow everything in our field of awareness to just be, even as we are interacting normally in everyday living. We call this the dispassion stage. It is the stage of being completely unruffled by anything that happens inside or outside us.

## *Dispassion*

The condition of dispassion is one of the primary goals of self-inquiry. Those who are very enthusiastic and dedicated to self-inquiry are very passionate about developing dispassion. This is non-relational self-inquiry, of course.

Dispassion is not a doing at all, and is beyond self-inquiry itself. It isn't even a letting go, for it is beyond choice. Dispassion is a state of being. It is the subject (the witness, our sense of self) developing through an integration of practices to the point where all the objects of experience are taken in stride, without identification. This applies to events, relationships, and all that is going on in the body, heart and mind.

Is Dispassion a state of indifference, a state of uncaring? Does it mean that we do not act or react in the world? It does not mean that. It is just the opposite. Much spiritual development is paradoxical, where less is more.

The gradual emergence of dispassion means we are becoming freer to act for the good of all. Inner silence will move to do this through us more and more, the further we travel along the track. It is the paradox of enlightenment. The more we have gone beyond, the more engaged we will become for the benefit of others. This is the nature of divine consciousness.

We really have to give credit where credit is due. Deep meditation (if we are doing that) is the primary cultivator of dispassion, because dispassion is an advanced stage of witness. A stand-alone track of self-inquiry can lead to dispassion also, but it is rare. To succeed, self-inquiry must ascend to the level of meditation, the transcendence of all objects of attention. If self-inquiry is done like this over-time, then the witness will dawn and, consequently, there will be dispassion. It is a difficult path, because it lacks a structured and efficient routine of practice (like deep meditation twice daily). The concept of practice itself may be lacking. Self-inquiry of the standalone variety will be about constantly remembering to disregard/release all objects of perception, including all thoughts, feelings and perceptions about external objects. When self-inquiry becomes a deeply ingrained habit, then it becomes a kind of ongoing meditation. How an approach like this will fit into daily life is another question, since it requires ongoing self-inquiry to be incorporated into every nook and cranny of our daily life. This may not be practical for someone with a family and career. There can be direct conflicts, particularly before the witness is dawned.

On the other hand, if deep meditation is undertaken in a structured twice-daily routine, and life is lived normally, the witness comes up naturally as a support to family and career, and also as a support to undertake self-inquiry in a way that does not disrupt the normal flow of life. Deep meditation makes it possible to recognize the witness and self-inquiry provides the perspective in a way that does not replace daily life and activities, but enhances them.

Dispassion is at home in the marketplace, as well as in the remote retreat. It is all the same. The combination of daily deep meditation and gradually emerging self-inquiry provides much more flexibility for living and is a much faster path as well.

## Outpouring divine love and unity

No one knows what the true nature of existence is outside the realm of time and space. Yet, oddly enough, we can experience it directly. The reason we say "we cannot know" is because the reality we are all able to experience through deep meditation and self-inquiry is outside the field of knowing. It is That, and thousands of volumes have been written attempting to describe That.

In the end, the best we can do is say, "I am That". Then we can carry on with the many descriptions of That – pure bliss consciousness, void, Tao, God, Allah...

It doesn't really matter what we call it. That is as good a word as any, we are That. All that exists is That.

If it sounds a little impersonal, it is not intended to be. For That is the source of all love, compassion, goodness, creativity and happiness in the world. That illuminates us with these divine qualities, and is the source of all good deeds.

There is a misunderstanding that has been perpetuated by some teachers – the premise that becoming That is the only thing of importance and nothing here on earth matters at all. In fact, according to this premise, nothing here on earth exists. In a philosophical sense this may be true. We also learned it in high school quantum physics, yes? Yet, when taken at the level of intellect, it is one of the biggest traps for getting stuck in non-relational self-inquiry.

There is the idea that it matters not one bit what becomes of this earth or the multitude of life that is on it. There is a distinction between one who is truly enlightened and one who has created a division between themselves and the rest of the world through non-relational self -inquiry, enforced by a rigid intellectual view. With clear relational self-inquiry based in stillness, we can reject this out of hand. *Neti neti*!

The enlightened are they who remain engaged for the benefit of all, as That. Advancement on the path to enlightenment brings with it the perception that we can only be free when all are free, for we are one with all that exists.

The image of the long sage on the mountaintop, indifferent to the travails of the world, is fiction. If a sage is not engaged for the benefit of others, their condition will be in question. True enlightenment is the spontaneous outpouring of divine love, which is working constantly to uplift everyone. The sage becomes a willing and wide channel for That, which does nothing while doing everything.

So, while we often view Yoga and self-inquiry as a going beyond, never to return, it is not so. We can never leave what is here and now, for it is what we are in our own self. The journey of yoga, and self-inquiry, is a journey beyond all that is, ending in a return and full engagement for the betterment of humankind – a journey from here to here. This is the high knowledge, and its highest manifestation in this world.

"I am That. You are That. All this is That."

It is an unending outpouring of divine love, whose fundamental nature and fruition in life everywhere resides in the oneness of unity. It has always been That and it will always be That. The witness and self-inquiry lead to a direct realization of That.

## Honoring Our Nature and Where We Are

Everyone has different inclinations and tendencies about how to live their life. This is also true in spiritual matters. Each of us has our track already built into our own nature. All we must do is tread it. Easier said than done.

Advice will be coming from all directions, especially as our spiritual desire (*bhakti*) is rising. When the student is ready, the teacher will appear. More likely many teachers!

It is up to us to honor our nature and proceed according to wherever we happen to be on our path. This self-pacing is very important when undertaking any spiritual practice.

Self-pacing is particularly important when considering self-inquiry, because it is easy to fall into a non-relational self-inquiry practice that does not serve our best interest. This will be any self-inquiry practice that is not in harmony with our inner call, which is a direct expression of inner silence (the witness) coming out through our unique nature. Even with a strong inner desire to engage in self-inquiry, some common sense should be incorporated to regulate our efforts in a way that assures smooth and safe progress on our track.

Not everyone will be called to self-inquiry in the beginning. If our heart calls us to dance the night away for God, or to be engaged in service to others, what good will it be to deny the relevance or existence of these heartfelt urges within us? We can dance, and we can serve! Self-inquiry will enter into our spiritual life in a way that is appropriate for us, if we allow it to happen without forcing. We will see the transcendent unmoving divine playing in every joyous act.

On the other hand, if we are contemplative and quiet in our nature, we may be inclined to engage in self-inquiry more than those who are inclined towards a more devotional expression.

In either case, it will be wise to engage in daily deep meditation, so the witness will be dawning from within, no matter what our tendencies might be in life. That way, self-inquiry will find a fertile field upon which to manifest that which is appropriate for us as we go about our daily activities. Then we will be able to interpret the truth of the world as we are living it according to our own nature.

In general, it is not a good idea to try and live our life according to the dictates of someone else, particularly if our inner voice is telling us that something is not right in the circumstance we may find ourselves in.

It is also important to honor our inherent nature and inner dynamics as they relate to the process of purification and opening that will occur as we engage in practices. This is an essential aspect of regulating sitting practices such as deep meditation, spinal breathing *pranayama*, *samyama*, *mudras*, *bandhas* and so on. Self-pacing is readily addressed by temporarily scaling back on the time of a practice if symptoms of purification related to that practice become excessive and uncomfortable. With daily practices, the nervous system will go through a process of purification, and our job is to manage practices in a way that will sustain steady progress with comfort and safety.

Self-pacing for self-inquiry is a bit more complicated, because most of us will not be doing it according to a predetermined schedule. Chances are, self-inquiry will be happening either naturally in relation to the rise of our inner witness, or in a deliberate way that may have little relationship to the degree of inner silence we have. This might result in overloading and excessive purification and discomfort in using self-inquiry in either case.

Relational self-inquiry (with the witness) will tend to be less disruptive, even if overdone a bit. Even so, it will be wise to scale back on self-inquiry and do other things (like take long walks or other grounding activities) if we begin to feel out of our depths, displaced from our center, or overloaded. In the latter case of overloading in non-relational self-inquiry (with limited witness), there can be headaches, dizziness, disorientation, depression, lethargy in every day activity, and a loss of motivation to pursue our goals in life. In the case of overdoing non-relational self-inquiry, the symptoms can be very destabilizing.

105

So, it will be wise to keep an eye on how we feel while going about our daily activities. If our sitting practices are in balance, and our self-inquiry is relational or not excessive, then we will find increasing peace and joy in life and will be less inclined to find ourselves in a grip of suffering, even in adverse circumstances. If our practices, including self-inquiry, are not in balance, we will notice symptoms related to the extra strain we are creating, and it is suggested to scale back accordingly until we find smoothness in daily activities returning.

Everyone will be a little different in this. If we honor our nature and where we are on our path, then our progress on the way to realization will be steady, with fewer disruptions along the way.

## Self-inquiry in Daily Life

It is becoming clear by now that self-inquiry is trickier than simply doing our sitting practices twice each day like clockwork. We know that if we are engaging in deep meditation daily, then the stillness of the inner witness will be coming up in every aspect of our life, and this will open many doors for us. We will become more peaceful, more creative and happier in whatever we happen to be doing. This has been the experience of many.

Self-inquiry is not like this or at least there is not reliable evidence to this effect. What we do know about self-inquiry is that there is a lot of interest in it. Its appealing logic is a magnet for the mind. We also know that self-inquiry is something best done in-between our sitting practice sessions, which can be a small or large part of our day. With the rise of the witness, self-inquiry can be a natural thing as we go about our daily activities. It can be as simple as noticing what is true and what is not as our perception expands.

But many of us will be looking for more than that sort of natural emergence of self-inquiry, which is an automatic discrimination. The mind loves to analyze, and it is more inclined to hang on than let go. So, looking at the role of self-inquiry in daily living is as much about what it is not as what it is.

Much of what people are doing in self-inquiry in daily living these days is the result of what teachers have written and said. So, let's look first at the role of the teacher in this. Then, we can look at what actually constitutes self-inquiry in daily living, and what does not.

## *Teacher – pros and cons*

These days, there seems to be an abundance of spontaneously realized teachers crisscrossing the landscape. They are more than willing to share with us what it is like to see the world through their eyes, and many are naturally inclined to offer stand-alone self-inquiry approaches, because this is how they see the world – a superimposition of the unreal upon the real. So, from the point of view, all that is necessary is for everyone to make the distinction between real and unreal – the problem of ignorance solved in an instant.

Such teachers are sincere in their sharing, and they want to help us find a way beyond our identification with this world, beyond our dreams, beyond seeking itself. However, there is a difficulty in following what these teachers offer. We can see where they are and where we are, but the means for travelling from here to there is not always clear.

Spontaneously realized teachers may say things like:

"Let's go. Be here now. None of this is real. Keep asking who am I? Who is experiencing this? Know the world to be emptiness with no substance. There is nothing here and there is nothing to do. Therefore, spiritual practices are not necessary."

This is the classic advaita (non-dual) approach to self-inquiry and spiritual development. In fact, it professes no spiritual development at all. Only the un-manifest reality beyond the ups and downs of this life is regarded as real and we are That already, to the exclusion of all else, even the many means available to aid in that very realization.

While philosophically sound, on the practical level it is a narrow view, which contains more than a little irony – the exclusion of the world from an all-inclusive non-dual view! A growing throng of modern spiritual teachers stand as proof of the fact. So why are so few of us benefiting from this approach?

Assuming a realized teacher of this type has charisma and credibility, the result of this kind of teaching will often lead to limitation of the teacher, rather than cultivating of the realization itself. The buzz will be mainly about the teacher and not about the student. This may happen in spite of the wishes of the teacher. That's just how it is. To the extent real spiritual experience does occur in the student, it may be short-lived (and sometimes chaotic) if practical means are not offered to expand and stabilize it in daily living.

While there can be much inspiration in visiting and listening to spontaneously realized teachers, if they do not offer a structured and effective daily practice that can easily blend with the modern lifestyle, then the long term value of what they are offering will be open to question.

The truth is that the majority of advaita/non-dualist style teachers, past and present, have taught non-relational self-inquiry. Not because they wanted to, but because their students have not had enough presence of the witness to make self-inquiry effective beyond the initial shivers of instinctive recognition. Any rational self-inquiry that has been occurring has been a result of how much inner silence the student has brought to the table in the first place, rather than the particular brand of self-inquiry being offered by the teacher.

When it comes to self-inquiry, the magic formula is not found in the method itself. It is found in the degree of abiding witness in the student. And that is the product of the conduct of effective spiritual practices (especially meditation), either recently or in times long past and forgotten.

Many spiritual teachers miss this point, because they teach from the perspective of their own level of experience. This can lead to a situation like a master mathematician attempting to teach calculus to grammar school students. What good will the calculus be if the students have not yet learned how to add and subtract? If the gap between the teacher and student is not closed somehow, progress will be limited. This is the situation when realized teachers attempt to teach self-inquiry to students who have not been given the opportunity to cultivate the witness.

Self-inquiry is not rocket science. When the witness is present, self-inquiry occurs naturally as an effect, based on direct perception of the transcendental self (the witness) in relation to our perception of thoughts, feelings, and the objects of the world. To cultivate this kind of subject-object relationship with self-inquiry alone is very difficult. If it were not difficult, we would have many more enlightened people running around, and fewer people stuck at the feet of the realized, hoping for an awakening by osmosis. It doesn't work like that – not for long.

This situation is sometimes blamed on the student not being ready for the "highest teaching" which advaita/non-duality is held to be. While the philosophy and the realization itself can be said to be the highest, the teaching certainly is not. If the means for developing the essential prerequisite for self-inquiry are not being provided by the teacher, it is not the student's failing, but the teacher's. The essential prerequisite is the witness.

The highest teaching is not necessarily the one with the highest ideal or objective. All spiritual teachings aspire to more or less the same ideal – the direct realization of ultimate truth, or God. But there is a huge difference in approaches, and this is where the distinction should be made on which is the highest, not on the end goal which will always be the same.

From this point of view, the highest teaching is the one that enables the most people to directly realize the truth of existence quickly and easily.

The highest teaching is one that is most effective and accessible for everyone. This will not necessarily be the most structured teaching, but one that is flexible and facilitates individual expression while being solidly grounded in the underlying principles of self-inquiry, i.e. the establishment of the witness and its relationship with the machinery of perception.

It is vitally important for every spiritual teacher to meet their students where they are with practical means that are appropriate for them at their present level of development.

However, there is a greater integration of methodologies occurring across traditional lines currently. More teachers are incorporating meditation in combination with the methods of self-inquiry. It is a logical step, and one that is much needed to cover the needs of diverse students, and break the logjam of non-relational self-inquiry. It is not a great distance from non-relational to relational self-inquiry. It is only a witness away.

So, while realized teachers can provide a lot of inspiration, we need much more from them. Most important are practical means that students can take home with them for enhancing their experience in daily life. Then, the truth will be accessible to everyone, and can be directly perceived and further revealed through the natural application of self-inquiry methods in daily living.

It is important to recognize that no matter how much spiritual energy teachers may give us in the form of inspiration, inner stimulation, or intellectual knowledge, the greatest value will come from our daily practices over a long term. If they give us a routine that will carry us steadily forward day by day into a direct realization of our true nature, without turning our life upside down in the process, then they will have done their job.

It is the duty of all students to demand nothing less from spiritual teachers. If a teacher cannot or will not deliver effective means, then it will be wise to look beyond for additional sources of knowledge.

All teachings have benefit, but no teaching covers all aspects of the process of human spiritual transformation. So, it is good to keep an open mind, and be willing to make the choices that are necessary to move ahead. No teacher can make these choices for us. We have to take responsibility for our own spiritual progress.

The greatest teacher is within us.

## Practical Applications of Self-inquiry

We know now that self-inquiry is practical when it is relational, and not very practical when it is non-rational. What does that mean?

If we are inquiring about who we are (who am I?), or making affirmations about who we are (I am that), and these are only ideas making more ideas, rather than releasing into the actual presence of inner silence (the witness), then the inquiry or affirmation will be non-rational, and therefore not very practical. From this, it stands to reason that the level and kind of self-inquiry we are doing will, by necessity, be matched up with the degree of witness we have present in our awareness. The more prevalent the witness, the more far-reaching our self-inquiry will be, while remaining rational.

So, logically, the first step on a track of self-inquiry will be ongoing cultivation of the witness. In any effective method where self-inquiry is employed, some kind of meditation will be present, whether it be in the form of a regular sitting practice, or an aspect of the self-inquiry itself.

Once we have cultivated the witness, the next step will be to notice its presence. It may be noticed as a calmness – events occurring without leaving impressions as they did before, more happiness, a bubbling up of creative energy, increased desire to know the truth via more study and inquiry. Or we may notice a silent wakefulness in-between our waking thoughts, during dreaming while we are asleep, or while we are in dreamless deep sleep. Any or all of these.

Once we have noticed the witness, we may still find the absolute philosophical tenet of non-duality to be quite foreign – the idea that there is only That, and all that I experience in the world, and in my mind, is an illusion; unreal. Hammering on this idea will not help us much to see that it is so, though anyone is welcome to do that. It will likely remain non-relational for some time before the truth begins to peek through.

It is much better to continue with daily sitting practices, and then take on self-inquiry right where we are in more mundane ways. If we learn to crawl first, and then stand up while holding on to something, we will be much less likely to fall flat on our face when we try to walk. If we take it step-by-step, we will be running before we know it. At some point, we may find ourselves having the time to notice who is noticing. It doesn't take any time at all really – only the witness. It begins in the many gaps of stillness that occur in between everything that happens in our daily experience, between our thoughts, feelings, and perceptions of the world. Eventually, the gaps expand and merge to encompass our experience all twenty-four hours of the day. Then we notice our stillness has become the blank movie screen upon which the entire drama of life is being projected.

Let's consider the five stages of mind discussed in the previous chapter. When we get to the point where we begin to witness our surroundings, thoughts, and feelings as being somehow outside ourselves (see last chapter, stage 2 – witnessing), then is this not necessarily the time to drop our active engagement in the world in favor of asserting, "I am that"!

It isn't necessarily the time either for pressing hard in our every waking moment with the inquiry, "Who am I?" while noticing and becoming identified with the witness puts us in the position to discriminate between the objects of our perceptions and the witness (stage 3), it does not mean we are ready to jump straight into dispassion (stage 4) and full realization of "I am that" (stage 5). It would be nice, but it seldom works that way. For those who try and leap that far immediately when they find a taste of real discrimination, it can be a rocky road with a lot of confusion and non-relational backsliding. Or is it forward sliding?

Either way, instead of taking the leap, it will be wise to inquire about our daily experiences in the here and now first, and begin to find relational self-inquiry in them. By bringing in the witness through daily deep meditation and gradually taking a different tact in our relationship with our own thoughts, we can improve our effectiveness and happiness in daily living. This kind of self-inquiry has tangible benefits, and is worth doing. Then we will be on our way to a more ultimate kind of self-inquiry. There is a natural progression in it.

We all know how difficult it can be to change our life by thinking alone and some of us struggle with it constantly. It seems no matter how hard we try, our relationships seem to keep going along the same tracks, and the realization we are working to achieve may elude us for a long time. The reason is because we are wrapped up in the way we relate and pursue our objectives in life. In short, we are identified with the life we have been living, including our style of thinking and relating. Deep inside, we believe that this is who we are.

The witness is beyond these deep-seated beliefs, so when we begin to inquire from that perspective, the identification begins to unwind. Then, we begin to see beyond our dream, and can interact in ways that may have seemed impossible to us before. Freedom! It is very practical.

We don't have to worry about realizing the ultimate truth, because once we begin to get our everyday house in order with relational self-inquiry, the big picture will not be far from us. It is important to avoid over-extending ourselves. We should learn to stand up and walk before we try and run.

There is great truth in the advice that if we want to measure the merit of a sage, we should first look at their ordinary relationships, rather than at their mystical attainments.

There are a variety of self-inquiry systems and they fall into two categories:

- Inquiry about our daily interactions and activities, with the aim to live in greater harmony and happiness.

- Inquiry about the ultimate nature of existence, and who we are in relation to that.

To be honest, the various kinds of self-inquiry systems in these two categories will work equally well if the witness is present. If there is a grain of truth in them, the witness will know, and self-inquiry will be good. Even if there is only little truth in a particular angle of inquiry, the witness will find the truth in that as well. All inquiry for truth, whether on the level of everyday living or the cosmic level, depends on that kind of resonance with truth (with witness). The presence of that resonance in self-inquiry is what makes it relational and practical.

Not everyone is inclined to structured self-inquiry, using specific mental algorithms, or formulas. That is okay. Structured self-inquiry is not mandatory if we are cultivating the witness. Our ongoing desire for truth and presence of the witness will be enough to bring us to full realization in good time. In that situation, we will know the truth, whether we are deliberately inquiring or not.

Ironically, those who are the most enthusiastic about self-inquiry will often be those who gain the least from it. These are people with very curious and analytical minds, constantly testing mental algorithms, but perhaps with less inclination to bring the mind to stillness in daily deep meditation. So, there will be a lot of non-relational inquiry and analysis going on there, but very little relational self-inquiry.

There are numerous systems of self-inquiry that are offered in the spiritual marketplace these days. All will be effective if they are done rationally, with presence of the witness. And not one of them will be effective if it is done non-relationally, with thoughts manipulating and interacting with thoughts. For this reason, we are not laying out specific schemes of structured self-inquiry in detail here. The effectiveness of self-inquiry does not rely very much on the particular mental algorithm we happen to be using.

Therefore, it is not necessary to examine the many structured systems of self-inquiry in this small book. It will be easy enough to look them up and gravitate towards approaches that suit our nature. Or perhaps we will evolve our own way of inquiring deep into the nature of things in relation to the rise of our own witness consciousness. In self-inquiry especially, the natural approach is usually the best approach, because it carries no pretense. We can call it as we see it. We will know this approach to self-inquiry we are using is relational by its ease and effectiveness.

Until we have found our own way by direct experience in stillness, this book can help in understanding the underlying principles of self-inquiry, and put us in a better position to evaluate any system of self-inquiry, or any philosophy and its mental strategies for unfolding full human potential. In taking a wise approach by cultivating the witness first, we will be able to easily distinguish useful methods from those that are not so useful for us every step along the way. We will find the truth everywhere when we have the inner witness to see it.

In discussing self-inquiry here, we will make a fundamental distinction between how we regard our everyday experiences, and how we might regard the ultimate truth of existence and our role in it. These are different categories of self-inquiry directly related to the stages of mind discussed in the last chapter. Both are essentially about the same thing, and lead to the same realization.

## Self-inquiry for every day experiences

Once the witness is dawning, we will be inclined to inquire about many things. Naturally, it begins with our everyday thoughts and reactions to the people, things and events in our environment. Our reactions until now have been rooted in the many dramas we have created for ourselves over a long, long time. Our reactions will change as we develop the ability to see beyond our inner dramas.

It is a great gift to be able to come in contact with the witness, so we can observe our thoughts and feelings as objects playing outside our sense of self. The ability to view external objects and events with a sense of independence will also make a big difference. Then, we can question our mental and emotional processes about all of it, without having the extra baggage of feeling that it is somehow us. We can see our dramas for what they are – just stories that we have invented subconsciously to carry us through life.

But are they true stories? If we ask this lovingly when they begin to play, with a desire to know, in the stillness of our abiding witness, we will know the truth. Then, what is not true will gradually peel off, or dissolve. When this process becomes a central part of our experience, it is a huge liberation. It is the point where we truly begin to discriminate – making informed choices about what is real in our life, and what is not. In this situation, we will find for the first time that we are able to consciously reverse habitual identifications we have harbored for life.

Prior to the witness, we have been inclined to react in ways that are vested (identified) in our thought pattern and the associated emotional entanglements. The common term is mental baggage – all the stories and dramas we carry around with us. In fact, these patterns and entanglements are nothing but habits of the mind, which is a machine whose function is only to produce thoughts based on previous cause and effect. As long as we regard our thoughts and feelings to be us, and our dramas to be real, we will be caught on the wheel of cause and effect.

The primary purpose of self-inquiry is to lead us beyond the knee-jerk reactions associated with this unending series of cause and effect, replacing them with the unaffected observer, the witness. Doing this by rational thinking alone is very difficult, so we bring in the witness with the easy practice of daily deep meditation. This adds the necessary additional dimension of awareness that is beyond time and space, making effective self-inquiry possible.

When we are having negative thoughts, whether they are coming from inside, without any visible external stimulation, or coming in response to external stimuli, we can observe them, and inquire as to their reality. If the thoughts we are having are not in our best interest, we can release them into stillness and not act on them. It is a choice we have. Likewise, if we are receiving external stimuli in the form of communications or events that seems threatening to us, we can inquire as to the reality of the threat. But not if there is obvious danger. In that case, we do what is necessary to protect ourselves.

If someone's action creates negative thoughts in us, we can contemplate about the reality of our thoughts, and choose to let go of our reaction. We also have the option to reverse our reaction. Let's suppose someone says to us, "I hate you"! This may create a feeling of anger in us. It is not for us to try and change the expression of another as much as it is for us to change our own perception and reaction. This is important.

We cannot change everything in our environment by direct means. However, with the presence of the witness, our perception of everything in our environment can be changed by simple inquiry, release or reversal. What we will find is that, to the degree we are able to effect change within ourselves, our surrounding environment will be gradually changing as well. This is because our perception of our surroundings, including other people, has a direct effect on the quality they will reflect, not only towards us, but towards everyone. If a mean person feels that they are loved unconditionally, a result of our own internal self-inquiry, then it is likely they will be much less mean to everyone. But it is not for us to take responsibility for their conduct, or take on their baggage. It is our responsibility to attend to our own perceptions, thought process, and reactions. This is what self-inquiry of the everyday variety is about.

Obviously, if circumstances require immediate action on our part to preserve life and limb, or even a reasonable degree of comfort and convenience, we take that action as necessary. Self-inquiry is not necessarily the best course of action when a truck is bearing down on us. We get out of the way! Then, afterwards, we can inquire about the strong thoughts and feelings we may have had then, and release or reverse them.

Our habitual or irrational thought pattern may say, "See, I am worthless, and that truck nearly running me over proves it. Next time it will get me for sure. I was lucky this time."

If we inquire about that, we can just let it go into our stillness, and move on to the next thing in our life, making a note to cross at the intersection next time instead of in the middle of the block. Or, if the negative thought pattern continues we can ask, "Is it true that I am worthless? And if so, why?" The mind may offer an involved rationale for its conclusion that we are worthless, or it may be a mystery as to why we are experiencing such thoughts. Either way, we can witness that process in stillness.

We don't have to engage in the thought process if it is not in our best interest to do so. We can release an untrue thought, or take the opposite thought if we choose.

This is not difficult to do if our inner witness is present. It is the essence of discrimination based in relational self-inquiry. We can choose. *Neti neti* – not this, not this.

So, if our mind is telling us that we are worthless, we don't have to argue with that. We can recognize that it is just a thought, an object in our awareness, and no truer than the thought that we are very worthy. So, we can choose to be worthy, rather than worthless. If the mind habitually keeps saying "You are worthless," we can choose to release that thought every time it comes up. In time, it will lose its power. We don't fight with our negative thoughts, this only strengthens and perpetuates them. Self-inquiry is not about opposing anything. It is only about questioning the reality of our experience, and letting go. In the resulting stillness, we can favor the reversal of the negative thought if we choose.

There is no need for extra analysis, which tends only to build castles in the air, though we need not to be concerned much about that if the witness is present. If we build a castle in the air, it can be dissolved just as easily.

Detailed mental analysis can be great fun with the witness in residence, because, when we are truly awake, we do not become identified with our mental structures as we did before. We may become playful with our thought forms. They become quite transparent, and can be whisked away with a simple release into stillness once they have served their purpose. No castle in the air can survive long when seen from the perspective of the witness. If the castle stays there, and keeps getting bigger, this is the sign of non-relational self-inquiry. It will be wise to let it go and make sure that we continue our daily deep meditation practice.

The thoughts to which we give our attention will be sustained and grow stronger with us. The thoughts we consistently release, because they do not represent the truth of who we are or what we want, will gradually have less influence over us. True self-inquiry is a state of constant release in stillness, which occurs when we reach the dispassion stage of mind discussed in the last chapter.

It is our own energy that feeds the dramas in which we choose to engage ourselves. Our desire and the choices we make in stillness each day about our own thoughts and feelings determine our track more so than anything else we encounter in life.

The variations on this process are endless, but the basic mechanics are always the same. We observe our thoughts and let them go. We can choose a new direction by easily favoring the new direction over the undesired one. It is a reversal of ingrained patterns in us in which we can participate directly through stillness. Over time, we can release our old negative habits in favor of creating more productive and harmonious ones. Our energies can be redirected to a higher purpose. In this way, abiding inner silence and the rise of divine flow in us can transform our life, and the lives of those around us as well.

Much of this will be automatic as our witness increases in presence. We will naturally see what is true and what is not, and choose our course more wisely than we did before. Feelings like self-condemnation, guilt, jealousy and pride are gradually replaced with feelings of peace, energy, creativity, optimism and love. In short, contraction and unhappiness are replaced with expansion and happiness. The unreal gives way to the real. This is how the truth sets us free.

Over time, our decision to choose the higher road in our perceptions, thoughts and feelings becomes automatic, and the habit of negative interpretation (the inner drama) becomes less and less. There will come a time when the only thoughts and feelings we have will be the ones that are suited for the most positive outcome in every situation we encounter in life. Such is the power of the witness and self-inquiry in daily living.

## Self-inquiry for ultimate truth

It is human nature to inquire about the ultimate truth of existence. We all do it to one degree or another long before we have even begun spiritual practices in life. And we will inquire even more about it as our practices go forward and mature.

We have an insatiable urge to know who we are and what we are doing here on this earth. It is wired into every human being. All the seeking that we do in life, whether for knowledge, fame or fortune, is ultimately about finding our place in the grand scheme of things.

The irony in this is that we are far greater than any knowledge, fame or fortune we can possibly gather in this life. And at the same time, we are much less, for our true nature is that which is eternal and unbounded, behind and beyond all that occurs on this earth. The least (our awareness) is the greatest, and the greatest (this world) is the least.

The role of self-inquiry in knowing the ultimate truth of existence is very simple – or realizing it, as is often said. All that we must do is release our perceptions, thoughts and feelings, and what is left is ultimate truth. That which underlies all that exists.

Of course, it is easier said than done, because realizing the ultimate Truth means dissolving every mental and emotional habit we have deeply ingrained in us. If it seems like a high price to pay for realization, it will only be if we are premature in the pursuit. By premature, we mean charging ahead with non-relational self-inquiry without the witness. Without the evolving presence of the witness, self-inquiry of this nature can lead to confusion and conflict in life. It can result in the cessation of all other practices and a loss of interest in fulfilling daily responsibilities.

On the other hand, if the witness is present and becoming gradually more prevalent in our life through daily deep meditation and other sitting practices, then self-inquiry for ultimate truth will become rational,

and not a major disruption in our life. This is natural
self-inquiry arising about all thoughts, feelings and
experiences, both negative and positive. Even our
mundane and neutral thoughts are questioned. For
the practitioner of relational self-inquiry, the process
becomes joyful and never ending, like a game or a
dance. If it is fun, we will know it is rational.

The nature of relational self-inquiry with ultimate
truth is such that every thought, feeling and experience
is met with the silent impulse, "Who is experiencing
this?" even as life goes on in all of its ordinary ways.
There is no strain or fuss about it. It is very easy and
natural.

The inevitable answer to the question is, "I am
experiencing this."

Then, what naturally follows is, "Who am I?"

There can be many descriptions of who "I" is.

"I am Bob or Betty."

"I am these thoughts."

"I am the one who is here."

Each of these is inquired about in turn, until the
last vestige of objectivity has been dissolved, and only
the subject remains – the ultimate truth. Even the idea
of "I" is individuation, and that which is behind all

experience is not individual. It is only "AM" we could say it is consciousness itself, but we cannot know for sure, because consciousness can only be known in relation to something else. That is why some call the ultimate truth behind life emptiness, nothingness, void and so on. As we have been saying, in Vedanta and Yoga, it is simply called That.

Those who have the experience of ultimate truth may describe it after-the-fact as having been somewhere – awake, not asleep, being aware, but not of any thought or object. Blissful sensations, boundlessness and a sense of timelessness are often associated with this experience. Perhaps this is why the yogis call it sat-chit-ananda, which means eternal bliss consciousness. Such experiences, described afterward, are not uncommon for those who engage in deep meditation.

Those who are purists about self-inquiry may deny the existence at all. This is actually true while one is in the condition of ultimate truth (pure consciousness) where no machinery of experience is operating. Yet, it can be described afterward. So, who can say? Experience, or the lack of it, it will always be relative to the observer, the mechanics of perception, and the relationship of objects to the subject/witness. The purist would reply that there are no objects, no mechanics of perception, and no afterward, only the eternal condition of truth itself right now – the never-born and never-dying.

As we advance, the inquiry about dissolving our identification with objects will continue even as we go on interacting in time and space...or seem to be interacting. It is a riddle, "To be, or not to be? That is the question."

One thing that we do know – the witness does coexist with our experience of the world, and enables us to engage in relational self-inquiry. So, the riddle is not unsolvable. With deep meditation, the rise of the witness, and self-inquiry, we are able to bootstrap our way to the eternal infinite, the shining void that we come to know as our self.

Most of us who are engaged in self-inquiry would like to have it both ways – to be in the world but not of the world. It is a natural desire, and suitable to keep us on the track. This is the goal of all spiritual practice – to find freedom from suffering, even while still in the body. More than that – to find happiness and meaning in life.

Purists about self-inquiry seek to remain beyond the suffering of the world. As part of this, they may also seek to remain beyond happiness and any meaning that might be found in earthly life. The purist may not acknowledge the expressions of divine love that accompanies human enlightenment. The enlightened cannot help themselves and often go to great lengths to express divine love in order to teach others how to be free themselves. Even so, much spontaneous activity may be regarded by the purist as froth upon the ocean of emptiness. And, indeed, they are just that.

What remains when the truth is fully realized are desire-less desires and act-less acts of love and kindness. I call it stillness in action, or outpouring of divine love.

The task of self-inquiry is not to end thinking, feeling and action, but to become That which is beyond thinking, feeling and action. In doing so, thinking, feeling and action will go on, but the doer is nowhere to be found. For that one is beyond all doing. What remains is divine doing.

On the practical level, this end state can be cultivated with a full range of yoga practices, beginning with daily deep meditation. Self-inquiry then comes along quite naturally.

If self-inquiry is forced before the witness has dawned, life will be strained and confused, and the results will be slow in coming. If the witness is present, self-inquiry will be there on the practical level of living in a way that allows us to continue our involvement in daily activities without constantly questioning our reasons for being engaged in living. The reason will become clear enough as the witness evolves within us and we gradually come to realize who we are and what we are doing here.

Then, questions like "who is writing this book" or "who is reading this book"? will be answered in stillness, and we will just go on. If we easily favor the question in our stillness, the answer will be there. And we will know that it is stillness who is writing, and it is stillness who is reading.

## Pitfalls of the Mind

The mind is a marvelous machine, capable of performing many great feats of analysis, deduction and discovery. It is also the mind that enables us to create the sense of "I" within us, "I am Mary", "I am this body", "I am this mind", "I was born, I am living, and someday I will die".

The purpose of self-inquiry is to use the mind to question and transcend these assumptions that are associated with "I am ....."

When combined with the presence of the witness resulting from daily deep meditation, self-inquiry reveals that we are not our name, our form, or even our sense of "I". What we are is the stillness behind and within all that is being projected. So, the first pitfall of the mind is identification. That is, the identification of our awareness with all the minds that are projected out into time and space.

Indeed, identification may be the only pitfall of the mind. The mind has a tendency to ramble on about our life experiences, whether they be in the past, present or future. And the mind will paint it as positive or negative,

133

according to our mood. It is always about one thing – the mind wrapping us up in something.

Is this the mind's fault? Is there something inherently dysfunctional about the human mind? Or is it something else? After all, the mind is only a machine. Do we blame the automobile when it skids off the road into a tree? Do we blame the hammer when it hits our thumb? Well, may be some of us do. And perhaps that is a symptom of the underlying problem. If the driver will not take responsibility for the automobile, and the carpenter will not take responsibility for the hammer, who will? Likewise, if the inhabitant of the mind will not take responsibility for its actions, who will?

Who is the inhabitant of the mind? It is we who are aware, to whatever degree we are aware. The less aware the inhabitant of the mind is, the less likely will the mind perform as it is designed to, as a servant. Then, the mind will be more likely to operate as a sorcerer's apprentice, feigning leadership and casting a web of confusion over life. Where there is a vacuum of awareness (the witness not present much) the mind will rush to fill the void with the only thing it can fill it with – lots of thoughts and false perceptions, which are in turn translated into false perceptions, "I am these objects of perception . . ." rather than, "I am the subject, the eternal awareness interpenetrating all these objects . . ."

So, the first step in helping the mind get back to its rightful purpose is to make sure the inhabitant of the mind will be present and fully awake. This is the witness, and we know the prescription by now – daily deep meditation. With the inhabitant of the mind moving in and taking the reins, there will be steady improvement in the operation of the mind. As the clamp of identification is loosened, the functioning of the mind will improve all the way around.

But the full integration of inner silence with the mind is not an overnight affair. It takes time. Even with the natural emergence of desire to engage in self-inquiry, there is still a long road to travel to full enlightenment.

These are the kinds of pitfalls we'd like to address here, because they can have a bearing on our ability to sustain practice and continued progress on our track:

- Infatuation with or fear of spiritual experiences.
- Over-analyzing and over-philosophizing.
- Overdoing self-inquiry or other yoga practices.
- The illusion of attainment, or of having "arrived".
- Denial of the need to engage in practices.
- The non-duality trap – denying the world.

Such pitfalls of the mind can hamper a spiritual aspirant at any stage of the path. Advanced practitioners are equally susceptible to be drawn off course, perhaps more-so when visited by dramatic experiences of the vastness of pure bliss consciousness, ecstatic bliss, and miraculous powers of one sort or other. These kinds of experiences can rock the mind if inner silence (the witness) has not yet been cultivated to a sufficient level of maturity in the nervous system, enabling the practitioner to take advanced spiritual experiences in stride.

So, whether we are just starting out on our path, or are quite far along, cultivating the witness will be the best insurance we can have to guard against the pitfalls of the mind.

## Infatuation or fear about experiences

Spiritual experiences come in many forms and, if we utilize effective yoga practices, such experiences will always be associated with purification and opening occurring in us. When experiences come, we will be inclined to think something about them. How we regard them will be a function of our understanding of the processes of Yoga and the degree of presence of inner witness we have.

When experience is dramatic, when we are overcome with a large energy flow or a vision of our vastness and unity with all things, then we may become identified with the experience. A kind of infatuation can happen then, or fear might arise about what we have gotten ourselves into, especially if the internal energy flow becomes excessive, which can lead to a variety of physical and psychological symptoms – also referred to as *kundalini* symptoms.

If we have been approaching our practice from the point of view of our limited self, rather than from the point of view of the witness, we may become infatuated in a way that is similar to romantic infatuation. All infatuations do pass, of course, and in the meantime, we will be wise to favor our practice over the experience. When we are engaged in sitting practices, we can just as easily favor the practice we are doing over visions or energy experiences that are coming. If we are engaged in daily activities, then we can just carry on with our work, whatever it may be.

If experiences overwhelm us to the point where we become fearful that we may be losing control of our life, then it can be helpful to stay engaged in life, particularly in activities that are grounding. These are physical activities, and activities that are about helping others. At the same time, we can temporarily reduce the kinds of activities that stimulate spiritual energy flows, such as attending spiritual gatherings and too much spiritual practice. We have mentioned earlier that this temporary ramping down of spiritual stimulation is called self-pacing. Such regulation is a primary consideration where an integration of powerful practices is being utilized in a self-directed manner.

Infatuation will pass and fear will subside as inner purification advances and we find a natural integration of the divine within us in daily living. This is why it is best to carry on with our life, no matter what our spiritual experiences may be. Ultimately, enlightenment is about marrying the spectacular with the ordinary. What remains is spectacular ordinariness.

## Over-analyzing and over-philosophizing

Whether we are having spiritual experiences or not, constant analysis and philosophizing about our condition (past, present, or future), will not be of much benefit. In fact, this tendency is one of the most common forms of non-relational self-inquiry.

When an experience comes up, whether it is physical, mental, or emotional, we have a tendency to analyze it. It will be good to understand that taking this to the point of obsession is a common pitfall of the mind.

This doesn't mean we do not analyze or seek confirmation of our track in the scriptures and philosophies that have been written over the centuries. But if we make analysis or philosophy the object of our path, we will be veering off on a tangent that can undermine our commitment to Yoga practices and relational self-inquiry. When analysis and philosophy creep up to the point where they become an end in themselves, then we have entered into the realm of building castles in the air, which is non-relational and ineffective spiritual practice.

In that case, we can just observe and let go of the excessive analysis in favor of cultivating the witness in our sitting practices, and going out and living our life fully.

## *Overdoing self-inquiry or other yoga practices*

A common pitfall of the mind is found in the idea that if a little of a particular practice is bringing us some results, then a lot more practice will lead to a lot more results.

For example, if we have asked ourselves, "Who am I?" and a flash of inspiration comes, we might conclude that we should be asking ourselves "Who am I?" twenty-four hours a day, seven-days a week.

Likewise, if we have been engaging in daily deep meditation twice each day for twenty minutes (a balanced practice), and find a noticeable presence of the inner witness coming up, then we might conclude that meditating much longer and more often will be better.

In either case, non-stop self-inquiry or non-stop deep meditation, we will be stepping into a mental pitfall that can actually slow down our spiritual progress. Overdoing practices will only produce excessive purification and strain that will limit our ability to practice effectively until balance has returned.

Although, some teachers preach the possibility of instant enlightenment, that all we are is here and now, nevertheless, it takes some time to open up the nervous system to the greater possibilities within. It is a process, which can be accelerated in particular ways, but not on a flight of fancy that more is always going to be better. The path to enlightenment involves a process that takes time, no matter what methods we are following, and there are few shortcuts that can bypass the need for self-pacing in practices.

Rome was not built in a day; and neither is the process of human spiritual transformation completed in a day. If we are steadfast in applying tried and true methods over time, we will benefit from the result. The journey to enlightenment is a marathon, not a sprint.

## *The illusion of attainment or of having arrived*

Enlightenment, the direct realization of who we are, is unassuming and does not proclaim itself, except by compassionate assistance offered for the benefit of everyone. Conversely, where there is the assumption of attainment or of having arrived, actions can be distorted accordingly, leading to a rigid teaching, proselytizing, sectarianism, and a shift in focus from spiritual practices to the one who has supposedly arrived. It is a pitfall of the mind commonly found on either the side of the teacher, the student or both.

When consciousness is identified with the mind, there will be a great need to proclaim victory over the forces of ignorance. This breeds more ignorance, of course. There can be no enlightenment proclaimed at the level of the mind. The functioning of the mind can only be seen as a symptom of the illumination which comes from within, or the lack of it. We may conclude that an inner flow is occurring or not, but we can never proclaim with accuracy that we have arrived, for that is beyond the province of the mind.

By definition, both the cause and the destination of true self-inquiry are beyond the mind. It is the abiding inner witness, which never assumes or proclaims anything. It just is.

When there is some proclaiming going on, it is wise to ask, "Who is proclaiming"? and then let go in stillness.

## *Denying practices*

There are rare cases of individuals who reach what seems to be an enlightened state in this life with little or no effort in spiritual practices. It is natural for such individuals to promote the idea of enlightenment requiring no practices from their unique point of view.

They will often say, "There is nothing to do. You are there already."

It is like the New Yorker who mysteriously wakes up in Los Angeles one day, not knowing how he got there, and then calls all his friends in New York to tell them they can do the same. If only...

This kind of teaching is powered, to say the least. While the destination may be true, the means will be lacking for nearly everyone. So, when a teacher tells us that we need do nothing to reach enlightenment, and we do not find ourselves there in that instant, then it will be wise to review additional means that are available. In this case, the conclusion of the enlightened one is a mental pitfall (yes, they do have them), and to follow such a teaching to the exclusion of everything else is a mental pitfall for a student.

A common symptom of the illusion of having arrived can be a loss of recognition of the value of spiritual practices. It is one of the greatest risks for advanced practitioners – falling into the belief that our journey to realization is done. The next thought the mind will produce is, "I don't have to practice anymore." And wherever we are on the path at that point, that is more or less where we will stay until we wake up enough to realize that our spiritual progress never ends, and therefore the need for spiritual practice will never end either. Practices may change according to our ongoing purification and opening, but the need for them will never end.

The reason is because there is no such thing as individual enlightenment in the ultimate sense. As we approach individual enlightenment, we know ourselves to be all that is around us. Then, the condition of consciousness of all who are around us is seen to be our condition. So, we will not be fully enlightened until everyone is enlightened. This is why so-called enlightened people continue to work for the benefit of all. Their liberation will not be fulfilled until everyone else is liberated as well. And neither shall ours. There is much joy and fulfillment to be found along the way, as long as we continue with our practices, yielding ever-increasing expansion to the infinite.

## The non-Duality Trap – Denying the World

Sages may tell us that the world is not real, but a projection occurs via our senses and a perception of objects takes place through the identification of our awareness. On the other hand, it has been said that perception is 100% reality, and this is also true. Our reality is what we perceive it to be. But the sage will say that it is all illusion, and that if we deconstruct the machinery of identification of our awareness with our perceptions, we will find that there is nothing there at all.

Well, true. We learned it in high school quantum physics. But is this a useful view of our world? Can we continue to function with such a view when taken at the level of the intellect alone? Not likely.

While the logic of non-duality is impeccable, the assumption that it can be realized instantly by everyone is incorrect. Those teachers who disregard the perception of others (100% of their reality) and refuse to meet them where they are on the path will fail to help them. In fact, damage can be done by encouraging students to reach far beyond where they are without offering immediate steps.

We know that if we try to run before we have learned to crawl and walk, we will land flat on our face and may find ourselves in serious trouble with our motivation and ability to function in the world. For the vast majority of practitioners of self-inquiry, laboring to deny the existence of the world is destructive. While we can certainly find inspiration in the concept of oneness, to attempt to live that in the mind is a huge pitfall. This is because oneness (non-duality) is not of the mind. As soon as we try and live it there, we will find much of our life to be meaningless, experiencing a false rejection of daily living, and this is very unhealthy. This is non-relational self-inquiry at its worst.

The paradox in this is that the experience of oneness is highly meaningful in all aspects of life, and is the source of all love and sharing in unity. The non-dual condition is an experience of unity, a radiant love and joining, not an experience of separation – not a denial of the world at all.

If we engage in self-inquiry with the presence of the witness, we will not fall into the trap of denying life as it is. Instead, we will find ourselves coming more and more into the condition of becoming life as it is, which can also be described as being in the world but not of the world. This is real oneness, real non-duality. Not the divisive non-relational kind of self-inquiry that can lead to years of struggle and misery. There is a better way of affirming the sacred proclamation of the sages that "all are one."

## Self-Inquiry and the Limbs of Yoga

Self-inquiry is found in all systems of spiritual development. Wherever there is discrimination on the spiritual track, there will be self-inquiry. Whether it is relational self-inquiry or not is another matter, and that is the key question. Is the witness present when we are inquiring?

Some systems of spiritual development are philosophical by nature and teachers may subscribe to self-inquiry as a stand-alone practice in order to adhere to the strict tenets of the philosophy. The philosophical system of Vedanta is one of these, and its strong stance on the non-dual (advaita) nature of existence, and the non-existence of the world, may leave the practitioner with little choice but to declare the truth of non-duality, whether it is being experienced or not.

Vedanta means the end of the Veda (the end of knowledge). It relies on Indian scriptures such as the Upanishads and Brahma Sutras to make its case for the non-duality of existence. The case is philosophically sound, if not easily realized outright by the average student. Vedanta also relies on the Bhagavad Gita to support its assertion that existence is non-dual in its nature, and therefore the world will be recognized as unreal even when we are fully engaged in worldly activities. Fair enough.

Interestingly, the system and philosophy of spiritual development known as Yoga finds validation in these same ancient scriptures, even though Yoga is often regarded as a dual rather than non-dual approach. Yoga also subscribes to and has its origin in the Yoga Sutras of Patanjali, which prescribe a range of practices designed to bring about the very condition of non-duality (oneness) held by Vedanta as the ultimate Truth.

The remaining systems of Indian philosophy and spiritual development are equally split with regard to being considered dual or non-dual in their approach. There are six systems in all, give or take, depending on who is doing the counting. All of these systems recognize the unified nature of existence, just as high school quantum physics does nowadays.

This raises a question: if all the systems recognize the non-dual nature of existence, then which one is the right one in its approach?

The answer is, it depends what you are looking for. What is not often suggested is that all the systems, and their methods, can be applied together for maximum effect. If the boundaries between them are dissolved, then the best of all worlds can be realized – oneness. This will not easy for those with a sectarian streak, which is a paradox for those who may consider themselves to be staunch non-dualists. How can anything be separated from that point of view?

Yoga does not suffer from such conflicts, and happily embraces all philosophies and systems of spiritual practice that lead to the best results. At least the most effective yoga systems do.

Patanjali was so erudite in laying out his famous Eight Limbs of Yoga that Yoga philosophy is able to accommodate many approaches for cultivating the process of human spiritual transformation. He may not have intended it that way, but his all-inclusive model, reflecting the full range of capabilities for spiritual transformation found in the human nervous system, has turned out to be compatible with multiple strategies and systems. The eight limbs form a good checklist for considering the completeness of any system of spiritual practice.

Patanjali's eight limbs of Yoga include:

- *Yama* (restraints – non-violence, truthfulness, non-stealing, preservation and cultivation of sexual energy and non-covetousness)

- *Niyama* (observances – purity, contentment, spiritual intensity, study of spiritual knowledge and self, and active surrender to the divine)

- *Asana* (postures, and physical maneuvers)

- *Pranayama* (breathing techniques)

- *Pratyahara* (introversion of the senses)

- *Dharana* (systematic attention on an object)

- *Dhyana* (meditation – systematic dissolving of the object)

- *Samadhi* (absorption in pure consciousness)

There is an additional category of practice called *samyana*, which integrates the last three limbs of yoga together – *dharana, dhyana* and *samadhi*. The mechanics of *samyama* are closely related to the performance of relational self-inquiry, as is further discussed below.

Self-inquiry is included in the *Niyamas* (observances) in the firm study of spiritual knowledge and self, and is also woven throughout all of the eight limbs in the form of discrimination, where particular modes of practice are easily favored over the many forms of experience that can arise. Taken together as a systematic integration, the methods of Yoga bring realization of the same truth of non-dual oneness that is expounded in Vedanta. It is accomplished by promoting a gradual process of purification and opening within the human nervous system, leading to its highest expressions of abiding inner silence, ecstatic bliss, and the unity of outpouring divine love.

Of course, regardless of its logic, such a multi-pronged cause and effect approach might make a devout non-dualist cringe. But, as has been discussed earlier, if real (relational) self-inquiry is going to take place, cultivation of the inner witness via deep meditation, as a minimum, will be a prudent course. In the language of the eight limbs of Yoga, the witness in daily activity is abiding *samadhi* (pure consciousness). There are many names for it. We will know the witness when we see it, and are it. A rose is still a rose by any other name.

Just as there are those with a fixed view of Vedanta, there are people within Yoga who subscribe to a singular practice, or other narrow approaches to the exclusion of the rest of Yoga, and everything else. It is easy to get stuck in a mode of little progress when taking a narrow view in Yoga, Vedanta, or any approach to spiritual realization. It takes a flexible integration of methods to penetrate the veil of ideas, emotions and perceived materiality in front of us, to realize the eternal luminous reality underlying it all, which is our true self. Just as a broad view of the systems of Indian philosophy can be beneficial, so too will a broad application of the methods of Yoga be more likely to bring results than a narrowly focused view.

This is consistent with the goal of Vedanta—the realization of the non-dual nature of existence. With an ongoing intent to drop our imaginary boundaries both in perceptions and in practices, and a willingness to utilize the full range of tools that are available to aid in this, we will be on our way. It will only be a matter of determining what methods to apply, and in which order. It will largely be a matter of personal preference, and a logical application of causes and effects to find out what works best for us.

## Devotion and Self-Inquiry

No matter what our spiritual path may be, it will have its original ongoing sustenance in our desire. It is our longing for truth and a willingness to act upon our longing that is the root cause of everything else that occurs on our path.

It has been said that a prerequisite to enlightenment is the end of all desire. This is not entirely true. Without desire, there can be no track; no practice of any kind. Even if we deny the need for practice in favor of stand-alone self-inquiry, a desire for truth will still be necessary to keep us going in that.

Desire in relation to the spiritual track is often misunderstood. As we come into a direct realization of the truth of what we are, it is true that our desire for the ephemeral things of this world will become less. A reduction in this kind of desire is effect rather than cause – a tail on the dog is rising realization. Even as our worldly desire may become less, our spiritual desire will be increasing in kind. Exponentially, some might say. So, enlightenment is not about ending desire. It is about shifting it naturally to higher truth, until all desire is dissolved in the reality of oneness, which is experienced as an unending outpouring of divine love. Then our desire has become synonymous with divine desire, and continues on....

An intentional desire for the realization of truth is not only useful, it is essential. When desire is directed towards a high deal, and is sustained, it is called devotion. In the language of Yoga, this is called bhakti.

Besides the obvious motivational power of devotion inspiring us to take action on our track toward realization, there is an innate power of transformation in devotion that directly stimulates inner purification and opening, independent of any other action taken on our part. In other words, devotion alone has the power to open us to the truth assuming the ideal of our devotion reaches beyond where we are today. This natural feature of devotion is why it is the most prevalent spiritual practice in all the world's religions. Devotion to a high spiritual ideal (divine personage, icon, condition or concept) is at the core of all spiritual progress, regardless of whether additional methods are applied or not.

Of course, as soon as we begin integrating additional effective methods with our spiritual desire, our rate of transformation to realization accelerates. In fact, it is devotion that leads us to all additional means. Devotion increases the effectiveness of all additional means we undertake, whether it be deep meditation, self-inquiry, or any other spiritual practice.

So, even if we are highly orthodox in our approach to self-inquiry, denying all other forms of practice, we cannot deny that it is our desire that is carrying us forward, raised to the level of unending devotion (bhakti) to a high ideal. There is something that is leading us to the ultimate freedom of realization of our non-dual nature. That something is devotion, the unifying power of divine love emanating from within our stillness.

## Meditation, *Samyamaand*, Self-Inquiry

A prerequisite for self-inquiry is inner silence, or the witness. When the witness is present we have rational self-inquiry. And when the witness is lacking to the point where our self-inquiry is merely thoughts interacting with more thoughts, with limited connection between the inquiry and the native awareness which is behind it, then we say the practice is non-relational.

We have discussed the role of deep meditation in cultivating the witness, so the relationship between meditation and self-inquiry on that score is clear. However, there is more we can say about deep meditation as it relates to cultivating a key ability in the mind. We can say that in deep meditation we find the procedural seeds for true relational self-inquiry. What is this key ability?

Stated quite simply, in deep meditation we are cultivating inner silence (the witness) in a systematic way by easily favoring an object in the mind over all other thoughts and perceptions. This is done by gently favoring the object whenever we are aware that we have drifted off the object. The object is called a mantra, which is the thought of particular sound that is used with a procedure that enables us to systematically bring attention to its core in pure consciousness, beyond all thinking. The procedure for using the mantra is at the heart of deep meditation, and also at the heart of the rise of the witness in daily life.

The rise of the witness is also at the heart of relational self-inquiry. In fact, we can say that the dawn of the witness is the beginning of self-inquiry. The ability we develop by easily favoring the mantra, which leads to stillness in deep meditation, the same key ability we utilize in easily favoring the witness in self-inquiry.

As we continue to meditate on a twice daily basis, we are conditioning the mind to reside in stillness as an automatic habit, even in the face of the never-ending avalanche of thoughts, feelings, perceptions and actions we are engaged in. Developing this habit of being in stillness, even as we are active in the world, is also the essential objective and desired outcome of self-inquiry. Once we have cultivated the witness in this manner, we have also developed the key ability necessary for self-inquiry, which is being able to allow thoughts and perceptions to pass by in favor of stillness. We don't have to cling to them anymore, or the associated inner dramas we have created in the past, for we have found our sense of self, our home, in something more pleasing, more lasting, and more present. Pure consciousness – our own self.

*Samyama* is a logical stepping stone once we have become established in deep meditation and find abiding inner silence coming up. It is a systematic means for developing the ability to infuse every aspect of our thinking and action with the quality of the witness. In deep meditation, we refine the object (mantra) and dissolve it in stillness, thus cultivating the witness. In *samyama*, we systematically bring stillness out into all of the objects in our life and dissolve them in that way. Deep meditation works from the outside in. *Samyama* works from the inside out.

*Samyama* is dissolving the illusion of the material world by bringing inner silence outward via our intentions into our everyday actions. Just as for self-inquiry, some degree of inner silence (witness) is a necessary prerequisite for *samyama*.

As our ability to flow outward as stillness develops naturally in life, aided greatly by regular *samyama* practice, we find increasing translucence in the world, and we experience through direct perception that we are living as stillness in action. Then we come to see the world for what it is, an infinite field of joyful emptiness in motion.

*Samyama* and self-inquiry are closely related, as both are about the same thing – cultivating the habit of operating within stillness. As our experience becomes more pervasive (first by cultivation of the static witness in deep meditation, and then by cultivation of the dynamic witness in *samyama*), our self-inquiry becomes greatly enhanced at the same time, simply by observing what is before us through direct perception. Then, it becomes easy to let go of thoughts and perceptions that previously had hold over us through the process of identification of awareness with perceptions of external phenomena.

What we find with the advancement of our witness from static to dynamic is the ability to inquire relationally from within every object we encounter, because we have become every object by direct experience. Our "I" sense has both gone beyond objects and begun to inhabit objects at the same time. It is one of those divine paradoxes.

Deep meditation and *samyama* add a huge dimension of effectiveness to our self-inquiry. In fact, these practices make self-inquiry inevitable, for the simple reason that seeing is believing. We could say that advanced relational self-inquiry is a form of *samyama*, where we automatically release all our thoughts, feelings, and perceptions of the external world into stillness. When we see what the nature of existence is, we are easily able to discriminate what is true from what is not without hesitation. Self-inquiry becomes an instant and automatic part of our daily navigation through life, and we move quickly onward from discrimination to dispassion, outpouring divine love and unity. Then we are doing everything while doing nothing!

## *Kundalini* and self-inquiry

The word *kundalini* and the phenomena it describes have received much fanfare and notoriety. If we are developing a serious approach to self-inquiry, even when recognizing the essential roles of our devotion, deep meditation and *samyama*, we may be tempted to ignore the thing called *kundalini*, because it is so deeply associated with the body. Of all the aspects of Yoga, *kundalini* is the part that seems to be most deeply rooted in the duality of existence, and therefore of least interest to someone who is seeking to realize the highest truth.

Nothing could be further from the truth.

*Kundalini* is about the energetic development of our subtle neurobiology, giving rise to the direct perception of radiant oneness in our environment. While even this perception is ultimately transcended, it is a necessary stepping stone that all who are on the path will take. Even if the process of *kundalini* is ignored, the aspirant will still experience it as part of the journey to realization. If the nature of *kundalini* and its various symptoms are not understood, it can lead to delays in our development, because the risk of failing as a result of an unknowing distraction will be much higher.

Like self-inquiry, a smooth and natural unfoldment of *kundalini* can be facilitated by developing a good foundation of inner silence (the witness) early on. Once that has been done via deep meditation, then other methods can be applied to assure a safe and progressive cultivation of *kundalini*, the ecstatic energetic side of our nature that leads first to ecstatic energy flowing, and later on to direct perception of the transcendent shining radiance that is within us and everywhere in our environment.

This is important, because full realization will not occur until both inner silence and ecstatic conductivity have matured and joined with us. This is the essential neurobiology of enlightenment found wherever human spiritual transformation is occurring, no matter what means are being utilized, including self-inquiry.

Self-inquiry will not find its fruition until all of the associated inner neurobiological processes have reached their maturation and fulfillment. If we do not attend to them in a systematic manner, they will occur anyway, possibly in a chaotic way. If we have a choice (and we do), then a systematic approach will be preferred by most of us over an approach based in chaos. Not only that – systematic is much faster than chaotic, so it is an easy choice. If we want to be stubborn about it and ignore the inevitable stages of inner transformation in favor of a fixed philosophical approach, then we will pay the price in both progress and comfort.

Those who are truly able to let go will notice the energetic processes occurring within them and do what is necessary to optimize them for a speedy and safe journey into realization. Those who hang on to a fixed view will face the ironic situation of hanging on to letting go, to the exclusion of everything else, including the actual process of human spiritual transformation that is occurring.

*Kundalini* is a vast subject, which can fill volumes. We will not overdo it here. It is an aspect of the whole of our realization that should be taken into account, and is covered as necessary to support the overall journey. We will know it when we experience it and be much better prepared to move ahead rather than become stalled in energy distractions. Relational self-inquiry can be used to favor progress in stillness over the temptation of infatuation with the inevitable ecstatic energy experiences that will happen along the way. We can release them in self-inquiry, just as we can all identify with experiences we may be prone to indulge in.

Yoga addresses the energetic side of our development through *pranayama* (breathing techniques), *asanas* (postures), *mudras* and *bandhas* (inner physical maneuvers), and tantric methods (the management of sexual energy in particular). All of these are easily incorporated into our sitting practices and the normal conduct of our daily life, in the same way that self-inquiry is naturally incorporated when we find the witness coming up and know that we are ready.

It is all part of the same journey, and no part of it is favored over the other. Each aspect evolves in its own time, and we know that each step is the right one by its natural emergence and observable results. In that sense, all Yoga practices are known by their relational resonance with each other, our inner silence, and our everyday activities. We will know we are in balance if life is getting better, even as we are moving steadily into a condition of non-duality, which is no condition at all, of course.

Self-inquiry has a direct role to play in the unfoldment of *kundalini* as it purifies and opens us via the central channel, or spinal nerve, running between our perineum and center brow. It is an aspect of the key ability developed in deep meditation, discussed in the last section – simply to allow the *kundalini* process to occur as it will while naturally releasing our attention in stillness. This help us to avoid going off into flights of fancy when dramatic *kundalini* symptoms occur, which they surely shall at some time or other.

It is like all experiences in life. We gradually come to know them all to be waves upon the ocean of our infinite inner silence. The difference between *kundalini* experiences and the rest of our experiences in life is that *kundalini* experiences can be dramatic, involving a range of physical symptoms, large surges of inner energy and ecstasy, visions, sounds and other internal sensory perceptions. The emotions can also be affected, sometimes positively and sometimes negatively in the case of excessive energy flows. All of this will have a corresponding effect on our mind, and this is the way self-inquiry (rational – in stillness) can be very helpful. We know that it is all just scenery we are passing by on the road to realization.

While the scenery is not important in itself, it does have relevance for gauging our speed and comfort on the path. If we are going too fast (too heavy on practices) then the symptoms of purification can become intense, causing us considerable discomfort and/or potential distraction. The process of introversion of sensory perceptions (*pratyahara*) can be moving too fast sometimes. It is important for us to be inquiring about the intensity of our experiences, so we can make adjustments in practices to maintain smooth progress with safety. If we don't do this, we can end up overdoing to the point where we will not able to practice at all for a while. Then, we will have to implement the appropriate *kundalini* remedies and wait until balance is reestablished again before resuming practices (including self-inquiry), which can take valuable time.

We have called this process of gauging the intensity of experiencing and scaling our practices accordingly, self-pacing. It is an important part and is also an aspect of self-inquiry. We always favor the practice over the experience and scale our practice according to the intensity of the experience, as needed.

The energetic/*kundalini* side of the process of human spiritual transformation is an aspect that is best not ignored. And neither should it be over-indulged in.

## *Yama, Niyama* and Self-Inquiry

Yama and niyama are the restraints and observances, which are generally synonymous with the codes of conduct found in every spiritual tradition – the proverbial do's and don'ts'.

161

"Thou shalt do this."

"Thou shalt not do that."

But this common definition is an over-simplification, and even a distortion of what *yama* and *niyama* really are, and, for that matter, what all spiritual codes of conduct are.

What *yama* and *niyama* describe are the behaviors that are inherent in our rising spiritual awareness. With effective spiritual practices in place, these are found to be effects more-so than causes of spiritual progress.

It has long been believed that conducts constitute a primary path for promoting human spiritual transformation, and this is why there has been so much emphasis on following rules in spiritual traditions for centuries. Yet, there are countless examples of people who have devoted their lives to good spiritual conduct and works, only to find at the end that they were little closer to divine realization than they were at the beginning. So, something has been missing.

There is certainly practical value in enforcing some standards of conduct in society, particularly in the area of how our actions might harm others. Otherwise, there would be powerlessness and mayhem throughout the world. However, placing a singular focus on spiritual conduct is a poor way to promote spiritual progress.

Self-inquiry is also a form of conduct, no matter which form of it we happen to be using – the "everyday living" variety, or the "focus on ultimate truth" variety. In fact, all of the restraints and observances rely on discriminations (an aspect of self-inquiry) for their performance. In any form of self-inquiry, we are choosing a particular conduct in thought, not just as a practice we do at predetermined times, but eventually as a natural habit in every waking moment. It can only work if it is relational – flying on the wings of our inner witness.

Perhaps over a long period of time, we can elevate a stand-alone self-inquiry practice to the level of an automatic habit. Perhaps we can accomplish this by living strictly according to the rules of conduct. But we must ask ourselves if we are only developing habits in thought or if are we developing habits in stillness? There is a big difference between thinking about letting go of a tendency toward undesired conduct and actually letting go of the tendency. Letting go can only be accomplished in the presence of the witness, and that is relational self-inquiry. Thoughts letting go into more thoughts is non-relational self-inquiry.

A shift from non-relational to relational inquiry happens in *yama* and *niyama* as we develop spiritually. So, we must ask, are we engaged in spiritual behaviors? Or are we engaged in them because we are moved from within our inner silence to do so? Behavior for the sake of behavior (for the sake of rules) is non-relational, though sometimes necessary to protect us from harm. Behavior for the sake of the divine flow of stillness is relational, and eventually supports the positive flow of evolution everywhere.

This is not to say we do not pursue behaviors we know to be right. The very desire to do is a sign of rising realization. We may find that this urge occurs more so as we find the witness to be more present in our daily life. It is deep meditation that is actually the fountainhead of spiritual conduct, because it is the primary means for cultivating the witness.

We can, therefore, consider the manifestation of spiritual conduct and the rise of relational self-inquiry to be aspects of the same dynamics in our lives, with both being intertwined with and a direct result of the dawn of the witness.

This underlying principal applies in every area of life, whether we are considering what to do in our career, how to handle our relationships, what to eat, or what Yoga practices to undertake. All of these things involve choices and contain self-inquiry. We should be considering them from the point of the witness, rather than according to the rules of conduct.

While some may argue that we have spread self-inquiry out into too many aspects of spiritual practice, it is all for practicability. The uncompromising practitioners of self-inquiry for ultimate truth will release all of this for the sake of the non-dual one, which is beyond the external veneer of existence and all of these considerations. Yet, even the absolutist in non-dual self-inquiry must get up in the morning, get dressed, eat, and relate to those who come around. Maybe such a one is beyond the trivial considerations of everyone else who is on the path. But will that be helpful to any but the few who have also transcended the need to navigate through the process of spiritual transformation?

Certainly, an end view is important, but it will be the real view only for those who are living it already. For everyone else, effective means are necessary. It is much better to take an airplane from New-York to Los Angeles than to try and wish ourselves there.

So, we take self-inquiry for all it is worth on every level, in every nook and cranny of the process of human spiritual transformation. We allow self-inquiry to function fully in concert with the effective methods of integrated Yoga practice.

## The End of Suffering – pain is inevitable but suffering is optional

Before we can consider what constitutes the end of suffering, we will need a practical understanding of what it is.

## What is suffering?

It is our identification with pain. And because identification is a function of the mind, suffering will be conjured up by the mind not only in relation to pain experienced in the present, but also in the form of memories from past pain, the anticipation of future pain. For those who habitually suffer, good health and physical comfort may offer little relief, because the mind can provide an endless supply of past hurts to lament and mountains of worries about the discomforts of the future, none of which exist.

In fact, a person's health, material prospects and external quality of life may have little relationship to how much and how little they suffer, since suffering is the product of identification rooted deep in the mind.

Those who seem to have everything going for them may suffer more than those who may seem to have little. Identification with material wealth and worldly, achievements (fortune and fame) can lead to some of the most severe suffering – a dream of life that turns into a nightmare. Why? Because, in that case, we have hitched our wagon to the temporary thing of life. No matter how glorious they may seem, they will not last. It is the mistake we make in assuming that we are what we are perceiving. And we pay dearly for that mistake.

Suffering itself is painful, but there is a difference between the pain of suffering and the pain that comes to us from an illness, physical injury or traumatic event. The pain of suffering is imposed by the mind and can be reduced and eventually eliminated through spiritual methods, while we may or may not be able to avoid the pain of real-time events. In any case, if we are able to release suffering, release identification with what pains us, then the inevitable discomforts and calamities that occur in the ups and downs of life will lose their grip on us as well. When our identification with pain has been dissolved, then suffering will be no more.

## Who Suffers?

The next time we are in pain, physically or mentally, and feel that we are suffering, we might ask ourselves the question, "Who is suffering?"

If we are honest about it, we will find it is our interpretation of the pain that is causing us to perceive ourselves to be suffering. If we are making a value judgement without our pain, we will surely be suffering. We will know we are making a value judgement if we are asking, "Why me?" or are placing blame, being angry, or trying to get others to share in our pain. In all of these reactions we are identifying with our pain.

On the other hand, if we see our pain only as pain without coloring it one way or the other, it will still be pain, but there will be no suffering – no judgement about it, no lamentations, no past regret, no inner drama playing, no fear about the future.

When we see someone bearing pain in this way, we tend to call them spiritual. They seem to be on a higher plane of consciousness, and the pain of the moment is not touching them in a way that is seen in the mental reaction we call suffering. This does not mean they will not react to the pain with a grimace or by crying out.

Whether we have broken a bone or lost a loved one, we will feel the pain of it, and cry out. Going beyond suffering doesn't mean we will like being in pain. Neither does it mean that we should not do everything we can to remove our pain, and everyone else's. But, whatever may be happening, the scars of suffering will not be with us, not even in the next minute, if we have let go of our identification with pain. It all happens in the present and is gone...

But, again, who is suffering? We have not answered that question yet. We have only described the mechanics of suffering. When we identify with our pain and are suffering, who is experiencing that? Is it our external sense of self? Our body/mind? Is it our awareness behind all of that? It gets to the heart of what self-inquiry is about. More importantly, it gets to the heart of what the witness is about, because without the witness there will be no relational self-inquiry. And without that, our sense of self will be externalized non-relationally in thoughts, feelings, the body and our environment. The temporal condition of awareness will be at the location of the suffering.

Yet, is that who we are? Only if we are identified and habitually claim ourselves to be our external perceptions.

When we find our sense of self to be the witness, nothing will touch us there. We cannot suffer when we are That, no matter what the body and mind are doing. It is a fact that our consciousness does not suffer even when it is identified. It is only consciousness – that part of us that always has been. It does not change, only the veneer of thoughts, feelings and the material reality outside it changes. Inevitably, there is change in the external. But we never change inside, do we? So, who suffers?

The truth is that no one suffers, except those who are identifying with the suffering, and even that is an illusion – a belief in something that is temporary, a dream. Yet, it is very real to the one who is having the experience.

All of this is rather idyllic and will mean little to us when we are in pain and identifying with that experience. The same can be said of all who struggle with non-relational self-inquiry without sufficient presence of the witness. It is a tough slog. We do not intend to be insensitive about any of this. Whether we have the witness or not, we will feel compassion for all who suffer. Our humanity calls us instinctively to help others who are in need, and especially those who suffer.

The reason why spiritual teachers do what they do is because more than anything they want to aid everyone in moving beyond suffering into the unending peace and joy that is ever-present and available within us all.

There is only one condition that can save us from identification with the ups and downs of life. Only one condition that can save us from the struggles of the mind within itself. This is the witness, our inherent silence, which can be cultivated easily in daily deep meditation. Then true understanding becomes possible for us, and we find ourselves able to move beyond suffering, and wondering who has ever suffering.

The power of the witness with the clarity of self-inquiry playing upon it is a paradox and a mystery. Yet, it is more real than all we see in our external world of thoughts, feelings, and perceptions of the body and surrounding environment. The witness and relational self-inquiry are real because they make a tangible difference in the quality of our life. And what a difference it is!

# Transcending Duality Through Divine Love

Speaking of paradox and mystery, as we find our sense of self residing ever more deeply in the stillness of our witness, in the shining transcendent glory of pure bliss consciousness, something inexplicable begins to happen. It contradicts what we may have been taught and come to believe about self-inquiry and the non-dual nature of existence. Yet, it cannot be denied.

Stillness moves of its own accord. It moves as an outward flow of divine love from within us.

As it does, the quality of stillness is retained. We find that our life has become a never-ending expression of stillness in action. Our natural ability to allow what is happening in life to play on the screen of our silent witness, remaining unidentified with the drama, leads to a dynamic in awareness we could not imagine before. We find ourselves engaged in doing many things, without doing anything. We have no pressing desires. Yet, desire is functioning. We see suffering and move to relieve it. We see need and move to fill it. We see beauty and move to honor it. Life becomes a dance. All the world becomes our sacred temple, and we move naturally in That without moving at all. We are moved by divine love and by That alone. And there is no moving at all in that situation. It is stillness in action.

In this outpouring of divine love there is eternal stillness, and an ongoing transcendence of duality. This is what life is in the non-duality that is described in Vedanta and Yoga.

Some have claimed that this is the end of ego. Well, maybe by someone's definition it is, but it is certainly not the end of the human person. Rather it is the expansion of the person to the level of divine expression. It is correct to say that enlightenment is the end of identification and the simultaneous expansion of divine engagement. It is the ultimate example of less becoming more.

Even as we claim no part in the world, we will be very active in it. For this is the nature of pure consciousness and the enlightenment it yields – the constant expansion of stillness in this transparent existence, exploding it from the inside with love and goodness.

It is nothing new. It has been going on all the time, you know. In our realization, we are only coming on board consciously with a process that was always there and is eternal. We were only out of step for a short time while we were identifying with the drama of life, created like a dream within us. When we find ourselves to be the one behind it all, we see it for what it is – a process that always was and always will be. Our eternal nothingness becoming everything we have imagined in a constant outpouring of divine love.

# A Confirmation of Unity

Believing in the true nature of existence has value. It can inspire us to undertake the means for realizing that truth. This is why it is beneficial to study, at least until we see the truth manifesting directly within ourselves. Then we will know its attributes by our own experience, as seen from within our witness which is beyond all experience.

On the other hand, if we have never studied a high philosophical ideal representing the true nature of existence, if we begin a simple and effective practice like deep meditation for any reason at all – for health, for happiness, for more success in life – the result will be the same. Ultimately, our spiritual realization is not about what we believe. It is about what we become, and that is about the gradual purification and opening of our inner neurobiology. This is human spiritual transformation.

Having said that, we also know that the mind will come along. As the grip of the habit of identification with our thoughts, feelings and perception is loosened, so too will the external expression of these aspects of our nature become more peaceful and radiant. Then, we are able to inquire about the true nature of life and all of existence without a lot of mental struggles. This condition of peaceful radiance has sometimes been referred to as having a shining quality.

Paradoxically, it is the shining radiance, the movement of inner silence outward from within us, that brings us surely into a direct realization of the non-dual nature of existence. This is rarely discussed in considering a pure track of self-inquiry. Why? Because, pure Vedantic self-inquiry may mechanically discard the existence of anything outside the void of awareness. Even awareness itself is released, because, we cannot know it without a sense of "I", and there can be no sense of "I" if there is nothing that exists to comprehend it.

Nevertheless, here we are.

If we honor the appearance of our present perceptions, and the fact that we are behind and within these as the silent inner witness, then, in time, we will come to know that the realization of non-duality is the merging of two. Enlightenment is the merging of energy with awareness.

This little-discussed later stage, where stillness becomes radiant and active, results in all of our activities and experiences being penetrated/illuminated by moving stillness – shining, as it were. And we become very attracted to residing in That, for we know instinctively that it is our self.

This is the true realization of non-duality, which is a unification, rather than a separation of undifferentiated consciousness from the rest of life. Even as we reside in stillness, we will be active, and the qualities of the divine will be expressed in that way.

This is a confirmation of unity, and it will be seen by us and by everyone who is around us. Unity is the outpouring of divine love in everyday activity. It is not the appearance of it (behaving in a particular way), but the internal fact of it, which cannot be mimicked for long. No matter what anyone has ever said about enlightenment, what it is or what it is not, we can only know it in experience as an expression of our own inner silence, which to us will not seem like an expression at all. It is abiding, because we are forever at one with absolute stillness. And in this abiding, we are far more dynamic than we ever were before we came to rest in our own self.

It has been said that final enlightenment requires a confirmation on the level of the mind. Perhaps it is so. In the end, the reason we have self-inquiry is so the mind may release and allow what already is. It is to allow us to be what we have always been – eternal divine love. After the neurological transformation and the emergence of outpouring divine love, it will be the intellect which finally reaches the point of saying, ahhh...and release.

Then, we will be beyond relying on external philosophies or teachings. We will be describing unity in our own words.

By applying all available means in a balanced way, and by inquiring, we come to know the truth of the witness within, and the conformation of unity will not be far behind. We will find mind and the world dancing with joy on the surface of our infinite ocean of being.

We are That...

# Afterword

The universal mind choreographs everything that is happening in billions of galaxies with elegant precision and unfaltering intelligence. Its intelligence permeates every fiber of existence – from the atom to the cosmos. And this intelligence operates through the seven spiritual powers. When we pay attention to these powers and practice the steps outlined in this book, we can manifest anything we want – all the affluence and success that we desire. Life becomes more joyful and abundant in every way, for these powers are also the spiritual powers of life that make living worthwhile.

More people than ever have undertaken a spiritual path of their own, independently of organized religion. "I'm not religious, but I'm spiritual" has become a common expression, and I count myself among those who struck out on their own as a seeker. My search has covered a lot of ground over the years, from human psyche, cognitive behavior, emotive techniques, higher consciousness and personal transformation.

What all of these disparate topics have in common is reality, in the sense that everyday reality is hiding from view, from the "real" reality that needs to be unveiled.

The physical and behavioral sciences are about the external world, while another hidden reality, which is crucial to spiritual seeking, takes place "in here," where the mind is the explorer and the territory being explored. This sounds like a contradiction, and so does the traditional way of reaching higher consciousness, which is called "the trackless track." How can you unveil reality "in here" when the explorer—the mind—isn't separate from the territory it wants to explore. The difficulty emerges clearly if you ask a question like "What do I think about thinking?" or "Am I aware of awareness?"

At best, these questions sound circular, like a snake biting its tail. But the contradiction is straightened out, and the trackless track makes sense, when you realize one simple thing: The active mind isn't the same as the still, quiet mind. Every method of spiritual seeking, if it is successful, goes beyond the active mind and its restless baggage of sensations, images, feelings, and thoughts, with the aim of settling down into pure, undisturbed awareness. As an analogy, think of the way in which one dives below the churning surface of a raging river, moving through deeper waters where the currents are slower, until one reaches the bottom, where the river is almost motionless.

Here, however, the analogy breaks down, because meditation, which is like an inner dive, can reach the zero point of no motion or activity of any kind. At the source of your awareness you can encounter pure awareness. Why is this experience worthwhile? Because the field of pure awareness is the origin of traits that are innate in us: Intelligence, creativity, evolution, love, and self-awareness are chief among these.

The trackless track makes sense for that reason. It leads you, without going anywhere, to a deeper level of awareness. Once you experience the deeper level, you find that there's a shift. You identify less with your everyday self, which is totally dependent on the active mind (along with the desires, hopes, wishes, and dreams it generates), and you start to identify more with the field of pure awareness.

In this way, higher consciousness gets assimilated into who you are and how you live your life. The word "spiritual" isn't mandatory to describe this shift. I prefer to describe the whole process in terms of awareness, which is a more neutral term. What baffles people is that the whole project of seeking gets tangled up in misguided ideas. Let me list the pitfalls one is most likely to encounter:

1. Mistaking the goal for some kind of self-improvement.

2. Assuming that you already know the goal.

3. Hoping that higher consciousness will solve all your problems.

4. Struggling and striving to get somewhere.

5. Following a cut-and-dried method, usually a method backed by some spiritual authority or other.

6. Hoping to be looked upon with respect, reverence, or devotion as a higher being.

7. Being tossed around by the ups and downs of momentary successes and failures.

I doubt that anyone who has honestly undertaken an inner journey is immune to some or all of these pitfalls. There is an enormous gap between where you find yourself today (totally dependent on the active mind) and the reality yet to be unveiled. Nothing less than an all-encompassing illusion surrounds us, a construct of the human mind that conditions everything we think and feel.

When it is put that way, the trackless track seems impossible or at the very least difficult and probably painful. However, I've listed the difficult and painful pitfalls. The illusion creates all the problems. It's crucial to see this. The actual track is effortless and pain-free. The mind by its own nature can know its source in pure awareness. By analogy, you can go through troubles, worries, everyday crises, and arguments with your children, but without a doubt you know you love them. Love goes beyond the other stuff—that's how transcendence, or going beyond, works.

The same holds true of the process of unveiling reality, which also goes by the simple name of waking up. The ancient Vedas declare that everyone is defined by their deepest desires. Desire leads to thoughts, thoughts to words and actions, actions to the fulfillment of desire. So, in a very basic way, the trackless track is a track of desire. If your deepest desire is to wake up, to escape the illusion, to unveil reality, and in the end to know who you really are, the message gets through. Your deepest desire activates a level of awareness that will lead you to the goal.

As with raising kids, the daily stuff rises and falls, but love, caring, attention, and devotion steadily work their way. The same is true of you the seeker, even though you are both parent and child to yourself, both teacher and student, healer and healed. Because these dual roles merge into one, the trackless track makes sense, and it works. As long as we require someone else to make us happy, we are slaves.

As you move closer to your soul, inward and outward become one. Old boundaries and defenses start to melt away. Instead of being cagey about the future, you flow with the river of life and nothing holds you back. The soul has its own devices, your intention becomes a blueprint handed to God, which He carries to completion in His own fashion; sometimes He uses a miracle; a personal dream may take the shape of reality or sometimes He makes sure you don't miss the plane to a destination. The fact that anything can happen is the beauty and surprise of the spiritual life.

# Further reading

Coomaraswamy, Ananda K. and Sister Nivedita. *Myths of the Hindus and Buddhists.* (New York: Dover Publications, 1967)

AYP Enlightenment Series, Yogani, AYP Publishing, 2006

AtmaBodhah, Swami pramarthnanda, ArshaAvinash Foundation, Coimbatore Boyatzis, R.E., Leonard, D., Rhee, K. and Wheeler, J. (1996), Competencies can be developed but not in the way we thought. *Capability,* 2 (2), 25-41.

*Bhagwad Gita* Subhash Vilas FP Publishing, 2006

Bar-On, R. (2006), The Bar-On model of emotional-social intelligence (ESI). *Psicothema,* 18, supl., 13-25.

Reichenbach, Bruce. *The Law of Karma: A Philosophical Study.* (Honolulu: University of Hawaii Press, 1990)

Ranachandran Rao. SK and Vaidyasubramanyam. V. *Consciousness in Advaita.* (Gandhinagar: IBH Prakashana, 1979)

Swami Vivekananda. *Complete works of Swami Vivekananda* (New Delhi: Advaita Ashram, 2012)

Edwin Arnold American/International Gita Society Bhagavad Gita Sacred-Texts Hinduism translation SBE vol. 8.

Gardner, B. R. (1984), Heteroglossia: A Global Perspective. Interdisciplinary Journal of Theory of Postpedagogical Studies May.

Gardner, R. R. (2002), Interpersonal Communication amongst Multiple Subjects: A Study in Redundancy. *Experimental Psychology.*

Gardner, H., *Frames of mind: The theory of multiple intelligences.* (New York: Basic Books, 1983)

Goleman, D. (1998), *Working with Emotional Intelligence.* (London: Blommsbury, 1999)

Goleman, D. (1995), *Emotional Intelligence.* (New York: Bantam Books, 1996)

Chopra, Deepak. How to know God: The Soul's Journey into the Mystery of Mysteries. (Running Press, 2001)

Kluemper, D. H. (2008). Trait emotional intelligence: The impact of core-self evaluations and social desirability. *Personality and Individual Differences,* *44*(6), 1402-1412. http://dx.doi.org/10.1016/j.paid.2007.12.008.

Nafukho, F. M. (2009). Emotional Intelligence and Performance: Need for Additional Empirical Evidence. *Advances in Developing Human Resources*, *11*(6), 671–689. https://doi.org/10.1177/1523422309360838.

Mandukya Upanishad, Swami Krishnananda, Sivnanada Ashram, Rishikesh

Mayer, J. D., and Salovey, P. 'What is emotional intelligence?' In *Emotional development and emotional intelligence: Educational implications*. Ed. by P. Salovey and D. J. Sluyter. (New York: Basic Books, 1997)

Mayer, J. D., Salovey, P., and Caruso, D. R. 'Models of emotional intelligence'. In, *Handbook of human intelligence*. Ed. by R. J. Sternberg. (New York: Cambridge University Press, 2000)

Mayer, J. D., Salovey, P., Caruso, D. R., and Sitarenios, G. (2003), Measuring emotional intelligence with the MSCEIT V2.0. *Emotion, 3*, 97–105.

Petrides, K. V. (2001), *A psychometric investigation into the construct of emotional intelligence*. Unpublished doctoral dissertation, University College London.

Petrides, K. V., Frederickson, N., and Furnham, A. (2004), The role of trait emotional intelligence in academic performance and deviant behaviour at school. *Personality and Individual Differences, 36*, 277–293.

Petrides, K. V., and Furnham, A. (2000), On the dimensional structure of emotional intelligence, *Personality and Individual Differences, 29,* 13–320.

Petrides, K. V., and Furnham, A. (2001), Trait emotional intelligence: Psychometric investigation with reference to established trait taxonomies. *European Journal of Personality, 15,* 425–448.

Petrides, K. V., and Furnham, A. (2003), Trait emotional intelligence: Behavioural validation in two studies of emotion recognition and reactivity to mood induction. *European Journal of Personality, 17,* 39–57.

Petrides, K. V., and Furnham, A. (2006), The role of trait emotional intelligence in a gender-specific model of organizational variables. *Journal of Applied Social Psychology, 36,* 552–569.

Petrides, K. V., Furnham, A., and Frederickson, N. (2004), Estimates of emotional and psychometric intelligence: Evidence for gender-based stereotypes. *Journal of Social Psychology, 144,*149–162.

Petrides, K. V., Niven, L., and Mouskounti, T. (2006), The trait emotional intelligence of balle dancers and musicians. *Psicothema, 18,* 101–107.

Petrides, K. V., Pita, R., and Kokkinaki, F. (in press). The location of trait emotional intelligence in personality factor space, *British Journal of Psychology.*

Petrides, K. V., Sangareau, Y., Furnham, A., and Frederickson, N. (2006), Trait emotional intelligence and children's peer relations at school. Social Development, 15, 537–547.

Pfeiffer, S. (2001), Emotional Intelligence: Popular but Elusive Construct. *Roeper Review,* 138-142.

Robbins, C. (2001), Developing leadership in Health Administration: A Competency assessment tool. *Journal of Health Care Management,* 188-202.

Rosenthal, R. (1977), The PONS Test: Measuring sensitivity to nonverbal cues. In P. McReynolds (Ed.), *Advances in psychological assessment.* San Francisco, CA: Jossey-Bass.

Sharma, Radha R. (2008), Emotional Intelligence from 17th century to 21st century-perspectives and directions for full research, Vision Journal of Business Perspective, Jan-March.

Ramanujam, K.M., (1937), Glimpses of Varaha Purana; Vol 1 Swastik publications

Rama R. P. *The Dimensions of Karma.* (New Delhi: Chanakya Publishers, 1994)

Sant K. Liberation *from Karma and Rebirth.* (Washington, D.C.: Temple of Cosmic Religion, 1976).

Chopra, Deepak. The Seven Spiritual Laws of Success: A Practical Guide to the Fulfillment of your Dreams. (California: Amber-Allan Publishing and New World Library, 1994)

Spiritual Initiation, Swami Bhuteshananda, Sri Ramakrishna Math Publishing, Press Mylapore, Chennai

Sankara and Adhyasa – Bhashya, SK Ramachnadra Rao, Rashrottamtthana Mundranalaya Bangalore, 2002

Spinoza (1677), *Ethica Ordine Geometrico Demonstrata (The Ethics)* Translated from the Latin by R.H.M. Elwes (1883)

Radhakrishnan, S. *The Principle Upanisads.* (New Delhi: Indus Harper Collins Publishers, 1995)

Chopra, Deepak. *Soul of Leadership: Unlocking Your Potential for Greatness.* (New York: Harmony, 2010)

Stephen-Knapp: Timings of Four Yugas, www.stephen-Knapp.com

Tattva Bodhah, Swami Pararthnanda, ArshaAvinash Foundation, Coimbatore

Thorndike, R.K. (1920), "Intelligence and Its Uses", Harper's Magazine 140, 227-335.

Venkataratnam, R. (1965), Self Enquiry –preachings of Shankaracharya, Ramana maharshi ashram publications.

Wechsler, D. (1940), Non intellective factors in general intelligence. Psychological Bulletin, 37, 444-445.

Wendy Doniger O Flaherty, *Karma and Rebirth in Classical Indian Traditions.* (Berkeley and Los Angeles: University of California Press, 1980)

Wright, K., and *et al.* (2000), Competency development in Public Health leadership. *American Journal of Public Health,* 1202-1207.

Yoga Vasistha Sara, Sri Ramanasramam Tiruvannamalai 2005

Patañjali, and Shearer, Alistair. *The Yoga Sutras of Patanjali.* (New York: Bell Tower, 2002)

www.ingramcontent.com/pod-product-compliance
Lightning Source LLC
Chambersburg PA
CBHW070535090426
42735CB00013B/2989